Creating Web-Accessible Databases

Creating Web-Accessible Databases

Case Studies for Libraries, Museums, and Other Nonprofits

Edited by
Julie M. Still

 Information Today, Inc.

Medford, New Jersey

First printing, February 2001

Creating Web-Accessible Databases: Case Studies for Libraries, Museums, and Other Nonprofits

Copyright © 2001 by Julie M. Still

Library of Congress Cataloging-in-Publication Data

Creating web-accessible databases : case studies for libraries, museums, and other nonprofits / edited by Julie M. Still.
    p. cm.
  Includes bibliographical references and index.
  ISBN 1-57387-104-4
  1. Web databases. 2. Database design. I. Still, Julie.

  QA76.9.W43 C74 2000
  005.75'8—dc21

                                     00-063283

Printed and bound in the United States of America

Publisher: Thomas H. Hogan, Sr.
Editor-in-Chief: John B. Bryans
Managing Editor: Janet M. Spavlik
Copy Editor: John Eichorn
Production Manager: M. Heide Dengler
Book Designer: Jeremy M. Pellegrin
Cover Designer: Dana Kruse
Indexer: Sharon Hughes

Table of Contents

Preface

Tip O'Neill, former speaker of the House, said, "All politics is local." Gloria Steinem, in the early years of the feminist movement, said, "The political is personal." And so, the origins of this book are both local and personal. After watching the circuitous route a locally produced database took on its way to becoming Web-accessible, and being tangentially involved in the early planning stages of this move, I looked around to see what printed resources on this subject were available for libraries, museums, and other nonprofits. The answer was "not much if anything."

Thus, this book was born, or at least inspired. The road to actual publication has been unpaved and more than a bit bumpy, but it's now complete. Edited works, as opposed to those authored by one person, are sometimes considered uneven, in part because a variety of voices tell the story. Yet, this is comparable to the difference between a group discussion and a lecture. It may be easier to take notes in a lecture, but a group discussion stirs up a lot more thought and is usually a lot more fun. The differing voices, overlapping sentences, and varying speech patterns and metaphors make the process livelier. In my instructions to chapter authors, I asked them to write casually, as if having lunch with a friend who asked how they did what they did or what they thought about the topic of their chapter. Other than that, they were left mostly to their own devices.

I selected chapter authors on a variety of criteria: a mixture of excellence of product, author experience, convenience, and willingness to participate. Most of the chapters are case studies, first-person narratives of moving to or creating a database on the Web. A few chapters concern some aspect of those databases, such as librarians' views of user experiences, cataloging problems, or coding languages used. For those who wrote case studies, I sent a list of issues to consider when writing. Not all would be applicable to every situation, but it would provide some guidance on what to cover. This is the list:

- Why did you or the organization decide to produce a database? Were any market surveys done? Was it something people had asked for, or was it provided because the in-house expertise existed? Would it be an ongoing commitment that needed to be updated regularly, or a one-time project with simple maintenance?

- Who did the planning, an individual or a committee? Did these people volunteer or were they selected?

- Who was involved in the actual production of the database? How were these people selected? Was any of the work done by students or outsourced? How were the students or outside agency selected?

- What problems did you encounter during the actual production? How were these overcome? If the problems were insurmountable, how did you adapt or go around them? How was your original planning revised after work was started? Readers will learn just as much from your problems (and your solutions) as they will from your easy successes, so please be honest.

- What equipment, computer languages, software, and expertise did you need to implement your Web site or document? Was it all available in-house?

- Were there any security issues you were concerned about? How were these dealt with?

- How did this project affect your department's relationships with others within your organization and with those outside your organization (if any)?

- How was your database initially received? What changes have you made in response?

- Do you keep track of who uses your database and how often it is used? How is this information used?

- What equipment and staff time (if any) is necessary to keep the database updated?

- Looking back now, what suggestions or comments would you have for others who are planning similar projects? What would you do differently? What would you do the same?

The chapter authors are very forthcoming about their problems as well as their successes. Readers may find the experiences and thoughts found within this book to be useful in their own institutions. Since technology changes very quickly, authors were asked to focus on the processes and people involved as opposed to the hardware, software, and other technical issues. Humans and institutions are much less mutable over time than bits and bytes.

I wish to acknowledge the assistance of a great many people in the preparation of this manuscipt, including those who contributed chapters, Frank Campbell of the University of Pennsylvania, my colleagues at Paul Robeson Library, Gary Golden (our fearless leader), and the fine folks at Information Today, Inc. They have been patient with me; listened to me whine, shriek, and vent; and told me the book would get done when I had doubts myself. I owe them more cookies than it is possible to bake in one lifetime.

Julie M. Still

Introduction

Julie M. Still
Paul Robeson Library
Rutgers University
still@crab.rutgers.edu

Most libraries, historical societies, museums, and similar insti-tutions have homemade files of some kind: a newspaper index, obituary files, lists of journals from a particular time period or on a particular subject, finding aids, bibliographies, and the like. Every place of learning has unique holdings and ephemera, but guides must be created to locate and use them. These guides are often cumbersome and crude, but they have saved the day on more than one occasion.

When the use of personal computers became widespread, some of these card files were transferred to a digital format, usually as either a text document or a database manager program file. They probably resided on one terminal somewhere in the reference area or in a back office. With the advent of the Internet, some of these files were trans-ferred to the network and made more widely available. The recent explosion in Internet use by the general public and the presence of PCs in many homes has made people much more aware of what is, and what can be, accessible from remote locations, and what can be shared among people in varying locations. The adaptation of com-puter and Internet applications to genealogical research is just one example of the way researchers—whether academic, professional, or amateur—have come to use and expect free (or for-a-fee) information.

Librarians and their ilk tend to want to give information away. "Information wants to be free" is a well-known rallying cry. Whether this is what draws people to the profession or is part of the voca-tional indoctrination is debatable. Regardless, those in possession of unique resources want to make them available to users—the lure of placing them on the Internet and making them available to the world is a strong one. However, taking a collection of WordPerfect files or an Access database and transforming them into a searchable or readable collection of Internet resources is not always an easy task. Even those packages that promise a painless transfer process involve more work than one might expect. Thus, this book was assembled in the hope that the experiences of those writing will benefit others planning similar projects.

The following chapters cover a wide range of topics. They are all related to Web-accessible databases, but, like the blind men and the elephant, touch on different aspects of the same topic. The chapters seemed to fall together into pairs (and sometimes trios), mirroring and enhancing each other when placed together.

We start off with Ronald Jantz and his explanation of the reusable platform he created for the different databases at Rutgers. He developed a way of transferring existing databases (or creating new databases) on the Web, and his work has made it possible for a number of researchers to make their data available to the public. He describes how the process works and how it adapts to the individual subjects and products involved. Reading this chapter gives an excellent overview of the methodology used in the rest of the chapters. Since he has done much of the actual coding, he can give a more detailed, technical (but very readable) explanation of the steps involved. Jantz's work has allowed the Rutgers University Libraries to make available a number of databases.

One of those databases is described by Vibiana Bowman. She writes about a locally created database of newspaper articles, press releases, and other materials concerning a specific locale. This is the sort of database (and card file) that most small libraries, museums, historical societies, and many other institutions have neatly arranged and tucked away. It's very useful but not very user-friendly. Finding a way of taking that information and putting it on the network so that it is available to the immediate population as well as the region provides an invaluable service. According to Bowman, the route from card file to computer file to Web database was not a painless one, but it might provide a road map for others wondering if that dusty old file might be revitalized and get more use if it were moved to the Web.

The next two chapters, by John and Mary Mark Ockerbloom and Melissa Doak, discuss their respective literary and historical Web sites. The Mark Ockerblooms worked on their own, as individuals, whereas Doak is part of a grant project.

Mary and John Mark Ockerbloom have created, with their own four hands, two wonderful Web sites. John's site, "The On-Line Books Page," is a metasite of electronic books (e-books), whereas Mary has narrowed her focus to "A Celebration of Women Writers," providing biographical and other information as well as the full text of some works. They discuss both the relative merits of and problems with working on their own as opposed to being part of an institutional project. It's clear that they each have the technical savvy to produce such works without a great deal of support; they also have a love of literature that drives them to spend so much time on these sites.

Melissa Doak is part of a team that has developed a history Web site with full-text documents grouped by topic, intended for use by teachers as part of class projects. It focuses on women and social movements from 1830–1930, and it was selected as one of the best sites on the Internet for education in the humanities. Doak and her team received initial and continuing grant support, which has allowed them to add more topics and documents and do more outreach to schools and teachers. With increasing usage, they are trying to plan for the future.

Two other history sites, one public and one commercial, present another comparison/contrast. While they both discuss similar projects, the difference in the locations and settings is intriguing.

Elizabeth Roderick writes about the wonderful historical databases that the Library of Virginia has made available to the public. The Library has digitized historical documents, records, finding aids, and photographs. Roderick's technical skills and knowledge of the process are evident, and her experiences will be of value to anyone taking on such a project. The section on the resources needed for such a project is especially interesting.

Her counterpart on the commercial side of things, Vicky Speck of ABC-CLIO, writes of the process involved in transferring two well-known, historical abstracting-and-indexing tools—America: History & Life, and Historical Abstracts—from CD-ROM and print resources to the Web. Given the excellent reputation of these products, ABC-CLIO was under pressure to make them available in a networked form, and to keep the databases up to the high standards expected by their users. This process is similar to the one any company, regardless of its size, would go through in taking a product to the Web.

The next two chapters also concern a commercial enterprise, but the authors write from opposite ends of the spectrum. One is a young man with a computer in his spare room and the other is a businessman with a gigantic network at his disposal.

Like many bibliophiles, Brian-John Riggs wanted to own a used bookstore and had begun acquiring books with an eye to achieving his dream in time, but a detour on the Web took him there sooner than he imagined. He discovered the ABE database, which allowed him to create a virtual bookstore by adding his inventory to the existing database and becoming a part of a larger system. Thus, he could avoid the overhead costs of a physical location, staffing, and the other bugaboos that sink many a fledgling enterprise.

Jeff Strandberg writes about 21 North Main, Inc., a front end for the ABE database that's geared toward libraries and other institutional purchasers. The company takes care of much of the electronic paperwork that institutions need and that small businesses like to avoid. His discussion of funding and computer architecture provides a unique view of the business side of things. Anyone contemplating a start-up venture would do well to read this chapter.

The remaining chapters offer a slightly different perspective than the case studies outlined above. There are some important and intriguing issues related to Web databases, not the least of which is usability and user reaction. Many libraries are struggling with the problem of cataloging Internet resources, including databases, especially those that are freely available and not under their control.

Anne Keenan and Laura Spencer write about the view from the other side of the reference desk. Keenan was the director of a public library in a small town near Omaha, Nebraska. Her opinions of users and their problems with databases provide some useful feedback for database developers. Spencer writes from an academic library perspective on the way the Internet has, for better and for worse, changed students' research skills and expectations.

Aurora Ioanid and Vibiana Bowman take a look at the cataloging of electronic resources in general and Web databases in particular. They discuss the concept of metadata and how it's related to cataloging schemes such as the Dublin Core. Their thoughts on full-text resources and the increasing need for—as opposed to obsolescence of—indexing and cataloging are very intriguing.

Richard Gartner concludes with a narrative on XML (eXtensible Markup Language) and markup languages for the future. He examines the current status of coding and indicates where he thinks it might be headed in the future and why. Those considering taking on database projects might do well to consider his predictions.

Readers may be tempted to start with chapters of particular interest, and I do not discourage this. However, a complete reading of the text will provide a more thorough understanding of what is involved in moving a database to, or creating a database on, the Web, as well as some of the related issues.

Chapter 1

Publishing Databases on the Web: A Major New Role for Librarians and Research Libraries

Ronald C. Jantz
Government and Social Sciences Data Librarian
Alexander Library
Rutgers University
rjantz@rci.rutgers.edu

Introduction

The paradigm for publishing is changing rapidly and dramatically. With the widespread and inexpensive availability of Web publishing technologies, anyone with basic computer skills can publish materials on the Web. The World Wide Web represents a technological discontinuity for libraries that will significantly alter both the way they do business and the role of librarians. There are many ways in which a librarian can respond to this challenge and opportunity. In a recent keynote address, Anne Lipow (1999) posed the idea that reference librarians are an endangered species and persuasively argued that we must change reference services in order to be viable in a technological age. She made some important points about transforming reference services so that information can be delivered "any place, any time." This article suggests another alternative for librarians: We can build on our skills of providing service and organizing information in order to publish high-quality materials, such as journals and databases on the Web, and thus provide additional options for meeting our users' information needs.

There are many very valuable databases languishing in research institutes, in professors' offices, and at reference desks in our libraries. As research libraries transform themselves into digital libraries, there are tremendous opportunities to publish these unique resources on the Web and make them available to the worldwide community of users. As database technologies become more powerful and flexible, librarians can combine their subject knowledge and information skills to make contributions to this dynamic new field of Web-database publishing.

In our efforts to date in the Scholarly Communication Center (SCC) of Rutgers University Libraries (RUL), we have worked with partners who already have established a database in some particular area. Our partners include teaching faculty, librarians, and institutes within Rutgers University. Database content covers an eclectic variety of sources that include information on topics such as alcohol studies, New Jersey's environment, journal and newspaper articles about urban areas, police in the U.K., public-opinion polls, and even knowledge management within the Library. In some cases, the databases were almost fully formed and in others they were under development or created specifically for a Web application. Many of the databases are dynamic in the sense that new content is routinely added as the subject specialists continue to work in their respective areas. In all cases, these databases had some serious access limitations (archaic access software, available only on CD-ROM, not accessible via the Web, limited search options) that led to a Web-publishing partnership between the SCC and the subject specialist.

Planning and Production: An Environment for Digital Publishing

Within Rutgers University's Alexander Library, the Scholarly Communication Center (1999, Collins, et al.) was launched in October 1997. It was designed to be a high-tech center that facilitated the use of electronic tools in teaching and learning and that used new technologies to enable the launch of digital projects. As a new and unique facility within the research library, the SCC began to make contributions by creating digital resources that not only demonstrated what could be accomplished, but also complemented the overall mission of RUL and the SCC. Given limited resources, it was not always easy to determine which projects to undertake. While Rutgers librarians, as members of the faculty, have considerable autonomy in setting their professional priorities, projects undertaken by librarians are expected to conform to overall institutional priorities. In evaluating whether to participate in the development of a particular project, the librarians and their partners were guided by both the mission of the SCC and project criteria as established by the SCC management team. The SCC's goals were the following:

- Provide opportunities to the university community for developing electronic resources and multimedia programs, and for handling electronic data, text, and images.

- Provide guidance, instruction, and training in the development, use, and evaluation of electronic resources in all formats.

- Deliver and publish digital resources in support of the educational and research goals of the university.

- Foster specialized projects using resources of particular interest to the Rutgers academic community and the state of New Jersey.

Although there are many opportunities to become involved in different types of digital projects, this chapter will focus on our efforts to publish bibliographic or reference databases. These types of databases generally provide searchable content resulting in the locating of a "document" either in digital form on a server or a print source located in the library holdings or in special archives. In almost all cases, detailed planning for these types of database projects was undertaken by a subject specialist and a digital project librarian. Subject content was typically provided by the subject specialist (e.g., a history professor, a librarian in the Center for Alcohol Studies, an art history librarian). The design of the Web site and database was typically undertaken by a digital project librarian. Students with a background in library science and/or technology frequently assisted in the organization of the database, reviewing the database for accuracy and completeness, and testing the final product.

Overall guidance and management of the database projects were provided by the library director and a management team within the SCC. Issues dealt with covered the gamut of library functional areas, including public access, copyright, archiving, cataloging, user interface, and the charging of fees.

The Concept of Reuse

Although the SCC provides significant resources and a technological environment for publishing databases, the process of publishing and the related system architecture are straightforward and can be readily replicated in any research library. A significant aspect of the process and architecture described here is that it is reusable. Reuse is a strategic concept for industry (Yourdon, 1997), and it offers many advantages to research libraries that are launching digital initiatives and that have relatively few experienced personnel or resources to dedicate to this new area. In corporate research and development (R&D) environments, automobile manufacturers describe common platforms consisting of the engine and chassis that form the basis for many different automobiles. In software development organizations, common components and object libraries can be reused to quickly produce different end products in which the majority of the software is the same. In the reuse environment, it is not only the technology that is reused, but also the process—the steps that the developer executes to create the new product—that is reused. Once the process and architecture (the reusable platform) have been established, these infrastructure components can be reused to quickly and easily publish many databases with different content that have similar technological requirements. The benefits to the library include significant improvements in quality as well as reduction in development time to bring a new digital resource online.

The Reusable Platform: The Architecture, Database, and Process

Our reusable database platform is relatively straightforward in concept. The underlying system and application-level components include a Windows NT server running Microsoft's Internet Information Server, ColdFusion, and MS-Access. MS-Access, a relational database system from Microsoft, is used to define the database and provide for database access functions through the use of SQL (Structured Query Language). ColdFusion (Allaire Corp., 1998) is a very flexible Web database-development tool that allows us to embed tags within the HTML files that provide access to the database through the SQL language. In effect, ColdFusion offers us a programming language and an environment for dynamically modifying HTML code that is sent to the browser. The ColdFusion application suite also offers a search engine that enables the developer to provide very sophisticated Boolean search operations on selected fields within the database. Although there are many technologies available today for Web database publishing (Perl, Active Server Pages), we have found that these specific tools offer the right combination of capability and ease of learning that fit well within our environment.

Through the architecture, standard Web-enabled user features are made available from common browsers such as Netscape Navigator and Microsoft Internet Explorer and include the ability to:

- Create or modify bibliographic records in the reference database.

- Search or browse using keywords or special fields such as title, author, or abstract.

- Perform Boolean operations within and across database fields such as "keyword" or "title."

- Limit searches using special subject and type categories such as primary theme, primary place, or document format.

- Retrieve the digital document either from the local server or from the Web.

Database Design

The reference database was designed to be as general as possible and yet not be overwhelming for the relatively small projects that we intended to undertake. We have tracked some of the key metadata standards in order to achieve a balance between flexibility and the standard approach. Our work originated with the Federal Geographic Data Committee's (FGDC, 1998) standard, which put considerable emphasis on geospatial material. We have since focused on a small subset of FGDC database fields that can be easily mapped to the Dublin Core elements (Weibel, 1997) or enlarged to be exported to databases that employ the full FGDC standard. We feel that this approach allows a maximum of flexibility and yet takes advantage of some of the benefits of a standard. A brief summary of the core fields and their relationship to the Dublin Core are listed in Table 1.

Generic Term	FGDC Standard	Dublin Core
Title	Title	Title
Author	Originator	Creator
Topic	Theme	Subject
Content	Abstract	Descriptions
Publisher	Publisher	Publisher
Date	Date	Date
Category of Resource	Document Format	Type
Spatial Characteristics	Place	Coverage

Table 1.1   Core Set of Database Fields

To this core set of fields, we may add special custom database fields that represent the unique requirements of the database. For example, in our New Jersey environment database (http://njenv. rutgers.edu/njdlib), we have special fields for geospatial information that contain latitude and longitude coordinates. In the alcohol studies database (http://scc01.rutgers.edu/alcohol_studies), we actually have several special themes that allow searching by drug type as well as physiological or social aspects.

One of the unique aspects of this architecture is the table-driven theme, place, and document format pick-lists. On the user interface, these pick-lists are used to enter data, search, and browse. Although the pick-lists appear in distinctly different parts of the user interface, the contents of each list are obtained from tables within the reference database. This aspect of the architecture enables the database publisher to easily create a domain-specific search process that is tailored to the information content of the database.

By way of illustration, the data-entry process begins by entering information about a document into the reference database. In addition to standard bibliographic fields such as title, author, and abstract, the user will also enter subject themes, places (if applicable), and document format type. The choices presented to the user have been determined by prior analysis of the information content to be contained in the reference database. To demonstrate the variety and flexibility of this approach, the process and respective theme tables are discussed here for three domain-specific databases dealing with alcohol studies, hazardous wastes, and the New Jersey environment.

Alcohol Studies
>   Alcohol—Diagnosis
>   Animal Studies
>   Detoxification
>   Drinking
>   Experiments
>   Drug Therapies
>   Intoxication
>   Lipid Metabolism

Hazardous Wastes
>   Dose Modeling
>   Lead Exposure
>   Metal Levels
>   Recreation
>   Risk Assessment

New Jersey Environment
>   Agriculture
>   Agro-Forestry
>   Air Pollution
>   Animals
>   Beach

Biodiversity

Botany

Buildings

The lists above represent the results of content analysis that have been undertaken by the subject specialist for each database. These tables reside in the reference database and are used to provide the pick-lists for the user interface. When creating a bibliographic record for a specific document, the subject specialist will assign one or more of the relevant terms from the respective table in order to describe what the document is about. Typically, a bibliographic record will have ten or more subject topics to provide access to a citation from many different perspectives and to enhance recall. Powerful Boolean operations are made available in the search interface to narrow the search and improve precision. When the database is being searched, the theme pick-lists appear and the user can easily select terms that will satisfy the particular search. For example, a user of the alcohol studies database might select "Drinking Experiments" from the Physiological Aspects pick-list and "Controlled Drinking by Alcoholics" from the Social Aspects pick-list as two themes and request all records that contain both of these subject terms.

The Reuse Process

The key to quickly and effectively publishing a new database is a documented standard process that can be easily used by digital librarians. The benefits of such a process include ease of training, a reduction in the time needed to publish a new database, increased quality from reuse, and less effort to maintain the published site. Given the architecture used, it is relatively easy to create another instance of the complete Web site and database. In this approach, the search process is easily modified by editing the theme, place, and document type tables as discussed previously. The steps of the process are as follows:

1. Create a copy of the Web site (including the HTML and ColdFusion code) and the empty database.

2. Modify the database description to accommodate fields unique to the new data source, or delete unnecessary fields from the generic definition.

3. Edit the ColdFusion code to point to the newly created database and enable access to the newly added fields.

4. Edit the theme, place, and document type tables to reflect the content and format of the new database.

5. Customize the language and the appearance of the new Web site by adding unique images, modifying colors, and providing the appropriate subject context in the customizable tables. For example, in the case of the alcohol studies database, the primary theme table includes entries such as drug therapies, medical complications, alcoholic beverages, cancer, and children of alcoholics.

6. Import or create new bibliographic entries in the database.

7. Based on the size and needs of the new database, attach a search engine to provide for Boolean searching of the database fields. This feature can be added through the use of ColdFusion and the indexing of special fields in the database.

8. Test the operation of the search process and enable access to the end product for users.

9. Document the technical details of the new site so that others can maintain and modify the site as appropriate.

One last step is typically undertaken if the Web site and data will be hosted on the SCC server and made available to the public. If this is the case, the subject specialist will work with a cataloger to create an entry in the Rutgers University Library online catalog. In this entry, the 856 field of the MARC record will contain the URL for the search interface. This step brings the new database into the library holdings and ensures that it is accessible to all who use the online catalog. The database also is announced on the RUL Web site under "News," and is added to the growing list of online indexes.

Recently, I have undertaken two new database projects that deal with hazardous nuclear wastes (http://scc01.rutgers.edu/cresp) and information sources related to alcohol studies. In each of these efforts, steps one through five took about 1 week of effort. For the alcohol studies database, some additional time was spent to streamline the process of importing about 50,000 records from the previously non-networked database and to implement sophisticated Boolean search techniques.

Research and Extensions to the Architecture

This section will cover some of the possible research directions that would enhance the architecture and capabilities, including the use of search engines connected to the database, automatic thesaurus generation, and searching across multiple databases.

Multiple Databases

One of the benefits of using a common platform is the user interface consistency and the ability to offer enhanced features across databases that have similar content. This aspect becomes very important as database publishing technology becomes more ubiquitous and more libraries undertake this type of responsibility. One feature of considerable interest is the ability to search across multiple databases. Vellucci (1997) describes the concept of metacatalogs and the need to develop tools whereby a user can identify specific library catalogs to include in a search query. This concept can be readily extended to the database publishing activity described here.

For example, a library may want to organize and publish a collection of interrelated databases. These databases might have originated in different organizations with different types of support processes, suggesting that it would be convenient to keep them as separate physical databases. However, if one uses the same platform and process as described above, it becomes very easy to search across the relatively small but core set of database fields that are common to all of the published databases. Although we have not implemented this particular feature with the collection of databases published by the SCC, it can be realized with a relatively small effort. For example, one could imagine a user wanting to locate resources on pollution in New Jersey. By providing a Web-based interface to select multiple databases, a user might select the New Jersey Digital Library, Eagleton public opinion polls, and the Camden/Urban Affairs database. All of these databases would support Boolean searching with a single query across the fields described above and would return results organized by database.

Boolean Searching

Depending on the size of the database and the user needs, it may be desirable to provide Boolean search operations. In the SCC, we have used the Verity search engine, which is integrated with ColdFusion 4.0. Within the ColdFusion framework, one can easily define a "collection" to be indexed. In this case, the collection is our MS-Access database containing the bibliographic records. Further, with a small amount of ColdFusion code, one can specify which fields in the database are to be indexed. In our alcohol studies database, we have indexed the following fields: title, author, and subject themes. The records in the database have been richly indexed with the subject themes and thus provide an excellent controlled vocabulary for searching the database. The search engine allows many powerful search options, including the standard Boolean functions and the ability to combine and limit in many different ways. For example, in the alcohol studies database a user might find an item from the special format field (Manuals), an item from the special population field (Children of Alcoholics), an item from the subject theme field (Drug Education in the Schools), and words in the title field (mother or father).

Digital Archives

With reusable platform architecture, it is relatively easy to extend the concept of a reference database to a digital archive. The extension is a simple matter of providing links in the database to digital documents that reside on the server. Although architecturally simple, this step should not be taken lightly. If documents are to be delivered online, issues of copyright and ownership must be extensively researched. If this major legal step can be resolved, other issues must be dealt with. In particular, the issues of archival ownership and preservation must be understood. If the digital documents come from a source outside of the library, the library publisher must understand who has ultimate archival responsibility for the materials. Lastly, if the material is not delivered to the library in digital form, it will likely require a substantial labor investment to digitize the collection. Scanning technology is readily available and relatively inexpensive. However, to scan, organize, compress, and deliver a digital document on the Web takes considerable planning and can soon become a labor-intensive process. Being able to put a few images on the Web can lead one to believe that providing a high-quality digital archive on the Web can be accomplished quickly and easily. This is seldom the case, and the scanning process requires carefully detailed steps to guarantee quality and uniformity.

The Challenges of Publishing Within a Library Environment

A research library encounters both benefits and challenges in undertaking a database publishing role. Although copyright and related legal issues appear prominent in the literature and are very important, it is the intent of this section to address several other relevant areas.

Archives and Preservation

Archiving and preservation is a fundamental responsibility of libraries, and the urge to preserve is endemic to our roles as librarians. The short-term benefits of digital information are immense in terms of rapid access, searching, distribution, and updating. However, the long-term archiving and preservation of digital objects presents significant technical, organizational, and legal challenges (Hedstrom and Montgomery, 1999). Paul Eden (1997) has provided an excellent definition of preservation that will serve to provide a context for our discussion. Preservation is "the managerial, financial, and technical issues involved in preserving (or archiving) library materials in all formats—and/or their information content—so as to maximize their useful life."

In the SCC, we have taken some basic short-term steps to preserve digital archives; however, we have not as yet addressed head-on the issue of long-term preservation. Both policy and technology issues are foremost when dealing with digital preservation. It is not possible here to address all the facets of digital preservation, so we'll examine this area from the perspective of publishing databases on the Web. As mentioned previously, our digital projects are generally undertaken with a partner that may be within the library system, or within or outside the university. In each case, it must be clear who owns the digital material and who is responsible for archiving the material. Typically, a library takes on the responsibility of cataloging the source and making sure that all the data are backed up on the library server. Within the partnership, it is easy for one to mistakenly assume that these actions constitute an archiving role and responsibility. So when undertaking the role of publishing databases, the library must explicitly address a number of questions:

- What is to be preserved? Is only the digital material to be preserved or are there original print documents that must also be preserved. Is the process (e.g., how the database was created) to be preserved?

- How long will the material be preserved? Frequently, the provider cannot specify a time frame other than the general "a very long time." If a database is no longer used, it may be taken off-line. Does one continue to preserve the archive as having historical value after it has been taken offline?

- In what form will the material be preserved? Frequently, digital libraries will have multiple formats, including a Web presentation format (e.g., JPEG), an archiving format (TIFF), and several intermediate formats (such as GIF) for thumbnails.

- How will technology obsolescence be dealt with? Over a period of 20 years, many computers and operating systems will come and go. Decisions must be made as to how to cope with such transitions.

- What are the long-term costs to the Library of archiving digital materials?

In the database publishing context, as long as the database is online we can generally assume that it is preserved in some popular database format. However, when we launch these projects we tend to forget that they may be lasting and heavily used resources that are accessed throughout the world. If we think in terms of 20 to 30 years, we will likely be confronted with serious technological obsolescence. In fact, it is probable that our operating systems and application tools will be upgraded and/or replaced several times. Therefore, we will be confronted with migrating the digital information from one operating environment to another. Certainly there is much uncharted territory for the library, and Jeff Rothenberg (1998) leaves us with some unsettling thoughts: "The vision of creating digital libraries—not to mention the preservation of human heritage—currently rests on technological quicksand. There is currently no long-term strategy to ensure that digital information will be readable in the future."

Digital Projects and Librarians' Roles

Clearly the role of a digital projects librarian offers opportunities for both librarians and the library. We must also recognize that many others are creating pieces of the digital library and that we must become partners with these scholars, technologists, and administrators in order to provide access to knowledge, whether it is has been languishing in the basement or recently created in the laboratory. Having many uncoordinated efforts will lead to a plethora of user interfaces that are hard to manage and that create confusion for the user.

There are some startling perceptions of our profession that should spur us to action. In setting up a database of electronic texts in astrophysics, Dr. Michael Kurtz stated that "librarians could not have helped us," and he indicated a lack of patience with the careful, methodical processes of librarians (Marcum, 1998). In one quote, Dr. Kurtz suggested that librarians do not have sufficient domain knowledge, that we lack an understanding of technology, and that our traditional skills are extra baggage that prevents us from doing our jobs effectively. As a result, libraries are in jeopardy of being left out of this new role of digital publishing. We do, in fact, have an opportunity to blend the careful, methodical processes of librarians with technology skills, and a familiarity with the scholarly material in a specific field in order to provide access to new knowledge.

The Future

This chapter has discussed database publishing initiatives at the Scholarly Communication Center within Rutgers University Libraries. So now the reader may ask, "Why undertake this type of work in a research library?"

All of the projects referenced have used some variation of the platform process as described here, resulting in a variety of content and types of databases that illustrate how we have been able to exploit Web technology. The process and the technology platform are straightforward and are mastered relatively easily, although this approach is not necessarily appropriate for all academic libraries. As mentioned in the previous section, the role of a digital projects librarian is becoming more prominent in research libraries. However, the library should be clear about its goals and what competencies are critical in the years ahead. Certainly, other approaches could be taken to deal with the databases described here. We could have used complete commercial packages and sacrificed flexibility and function with some cost tradeoffs (software purchases vs. salaries). We could have chosen to outsource the database publishing activity, clearly indicating that this is not a role or competency that is vital to the library. Finally, we might have chosen not to publish these databases at all. Our partners would have tried to find other publishing opportunities, or possibly these databases would never have been published.

In addition to establishing a strategic framework in a research library for database publishing, there are some very practical issues. Foremost is the fact that a reasonably skilled digital projects librarian can make a lot more money in the corporate world than in an academic library. This fact is a primary motivating factor for the reusable platform and process discussed here. Our approach has been to select and stabilize a platform that can be quickly learned and put to practical use. We have intentionally avoided more complex (and more powerful) technologies such as Microsoft's Active Server Pages. As a result, we have had many "digital project librarians" whose official title or position may be staff, temporary librarian, library school student, or computer science student, and who have all been able to contribute effectively to our database publishing activities. Given this staff profile, we must operate the SCC with a mindset that our digital projects staff will only be with us for a relatively short time. We are continuously in a hiring mode and always looking for ways to provide long-term quality support to our customers and smooth over the short-term disruptions that occur from frequent staff turnover. Hence, we must put a premium on efficient hiring and training techniques.

Library administrators must also consider what role publishing databases, journals, electronic courses, and similar projects will play in the future of the library. Libraries are not immune to the competitive forces in the marketplace. We are well aware of the price increases in journals, and there is considerable concern that publishers will soon start marketing their databases directly to the end-user (Majka, 1999). If publishers can solve the problem of delivery and pricing for a single user, direct delivery will be inevitable and will occur quickly. In corporate jargon, our libraries will have lost significant market share and our response should be, in part, to begin creating new products and services. Publishing on the Web—and the related skills and competencies—can not only put us in a better and more informed negotiating position with vendors, but this strategic direction can also help create new products and delivery methods that will assist us in retaining and growing our customer base.

These issues are all very practical matters. In short, our future will look nothing like the past. Librarians cannot easily extrapolate from current and past experiences to determine their future course. Given the impact of technology, we must close our eyes, imagine a new world, and be ready to take advantage of the opportunities it offers.

References

Allaire Corp. (1998). *ColdFusion 4.0 White Paper.* Available at http://www.allaire.com.

Collins, B., Fabiano, E., Langschied, L., Toyama, R., and Wilson, M. (1999). *The Scholarly Communication Center. Meeting the Rutgers Experience.* Chicago: American Library Association.

Eden, P. (1997). Concern for the future: preservation management in libraries and archives. *Journal of Librarianship and Information Science,* 29 (3), 121–129.

Federal Geographic Data Committee Standards (1998). Content standard for digital geospatial metadata (version 2). Available at http://fgdc.er.usgs.gov/metadata/contstan.html.

Hedstrom, M. and Montgomery, S. (January, 1999). Digital preservation needs and requirements in RLG member institutions. Available at http://www.rlg.org. Research Libraries Group, Mountain View, California.

Lipow, A. (1999). Serving the remote user: Reference service in the digital environment. Available at http://www.csu.au/special/online99/proceedings99/200.htm.

Majka, D. (1999). Of portals, publishers, and privatization. *American Libraries,* 30 (9), 46–49.

Marcum, D. (November/December, 1998). Educating leaders for the digital library. *Council on Library and Information Resources,* 6, pp. 1, 4.

Rothenberg, J. (December, 1998). Council on Library and Information Resouces.

Vellucci, S. (1997). Options for organizing electronic resources: The coexistence of metadata. *Bulletin of the American Society for Information Science*, 24 (1), 14–17.

Weibel, S. (1997). The Dublin Core: A simple content description model for electronic resources. *Bulletin of the American Society for Information Science*, 24 (1), 9–11.

Yourdon, E. (1997). *Death March: The complete software developer's guide to surviving Mission Impossible projects.* Upper Saddle River, NJ: Prentice Hall.

Chapter 2

The Rutgers-Camden Database: A Case Study from Scrapbooks to the World Wide Web

Vibiana Bowman
Reference Librarian
Paul Robeson Library
Rutgers University-Camden
bowman@crab.rutgers.edu

Introduction

What follows is a case history of the construction of an academic, noncommercial Web database that eventually became available to the Rutgers University Libraries system. Those involved in its creation discuss their first-hand experiences with how the system evolved, what they did that worked, and what they wish they had known before they started.

Background

The Paul Robeson Library of the Rutgers University Libraries System is located in Camden, New Jersey. Robeson Library is the main research facility for the graduate and undergraduate programs of the Camden campuses of Rutgers University, Rowan University, and Camden County College. Local public, private, and charter middle and high school students make use of the facility as well.

Camden, just across the Delaware River from Philadephia and home of the poet Walt Whitman, is also the state of New Jersey's poorest city, hosting the myriad problems associated with urban decay. There are, and have been for several decades, community activists and leaders dedicated to revitalizing the city. These community leaders also use Robeson Library to research materials for grants and proposals. Finally, since the library is in downtown Camden, it also serves the nearby courthouse, Federal Building, law offices, and government offices.

Along with the Camden County Historical Society, Robeson Library serves as a research base for local history buffs and amateur genealogists. Robeson has census materials and old phone directories dating back to the early 19th century. Its newspaper collection includes microfilm copies of regional papers dating back to the late 18th century. Among others, Rutgers-Camden offers programs in history, urban planning, and public policy. Part of the curriculum for these graduate and undergraduate students includes research papers and projects dealing with Camden, its history, and its future.

Thus, although Robeson Library is an academic library, its user base is fairly diverse. The campus has strong ties to the Camden community. In addition to its primary mission to serve the university's students, faculty, and staff, Robeson Library has made a commitment to support the community in which it exists.

The Problem

One of the most difficult topics to research is local history and news stories of local interest. Most often these stories are not covered in the major abstracting-and-indexing services since they rarely get national coverage. For example, in Camden in 1949, a World War II combat veteran named Howard Unruh went on a killing spree in his neighborhood. With twelve people killed and four others wounded, this event bears the grim distinction of being the first modern mass murder. While the story received some national coverage, the *Courier-Post* (the local daily paper of Camden County, New Jersey) covered it in exhaustive detail. Unruh (now in his late 70s) never stood trial and was committed to a high-security psychiatric facility. Every year for the past 16 years, one of the survivors attends Unruh's review hearings and recounts the horrors on the day of the killings. The *Courier-Post* still runs the story of the appeals process and recounts the events of the original tragedy.

Undoubtedly, this is a dramatic story rich in tragic detail and human interest. No national coverage would have the depth of appeal that local reporting has. But how does a researcher get access to this level of historic detail?

The *Courier-Post's* main competition is *The Philadelphia Inquirer*, a large metropolitan newspaper. While *The Philadelphia Inquirer* has a South Jersey section and does an adequate job of covering Camden politics and news stories, it does not cover these topics with the same depth or with the same frequency as the *Courier-Post*. There is no searchable index, neither paper nor electronic format, for the *Courier-Post*. Until the mid-1990s the users of Robeson Library did not have access to a word index to search *The Philadelphia Inquirer*. This changed when the library began purchasing the newspaper as a searchable CD-ROM, but up until that time, searching for local stories was a tedious task. Users had to obtain the date of the event that they wished to research and then spool through pages of microfilm. The librarians at Robeson Library felt there had to be a better solution to serve their user base.

As previously stated, the need for access to local history and local news stories has always been of prime importance to the users of Robeson Library. The problem that presented itself to the librarians at Robeson Library in the early 1970s was how to best provide that access.

Before the Dawn of the PC

Robeson Library was built in 1969. In the early 1970s, business librarian Tim Schiller began to keep a clippings file of local news stories of note. Among other things, the file contained stories about: student demonstrations on campus, gangs, political figures, political scandals, and education issues. General-interest items, such as birth announcements, obituaries, marriage announcements, and such were not normally included unless the story had some kind of special regional significance. The clippings were kept in scrapbooks loosely organized by subject and date.

As the files grew over the years, and as they became more cumbersome to access, Schiller began an indexing system to make retrieval easier. By the early 1980s, he began to periodically produce a computer printout of the file, which included the indexing terms and a list of citations. Around this time, maintenance of the file became the responsibility of the humanities librarian, Jean Crescenzi. The story now enters into the world of computers and "thereby hangs the tale."

Enter the PC

One of Crescenzi's areas of interest was (and still is) the history of South Jersey, specifically the city of Camden. Crescenzi served as the main resource contact for local grant writers, community leaders, and local history scholars. She was all too aware of the problems that existed in accessing information about Camden and the clippings file's lack of flexibility. In the late 1980s Crescenzi took an academic leave to create a database for this file in order to make searching it easier.

The first consideration was what software package should be used to produce this database. Theodora Haynes, now the business librarian for Robeson Library, had just completed a book, *Labor*

Arbitration: An Annotated Bibliography. In producing this work, Haynes used a software package called ProCite, a citation-management tool. At the recommendation of the library director, Dr. Gary Golden, and with Haynes providing the technical expertise, Crescenzi decided to use ProCite as the software for her database.

The reasons for the choice of ProCite were:

1. Robeson Library already owned the ProCite package.

2. One of the librarians was versed in its use and could provide support.

3. ProCite is a user-friendly database.

4. ProCite is easy to use for simple searches.

The Camden ProCite database, in its initial form, was very simple and fairly bare-bones. It did not lend itself to complex searching, since ProCite wasn't intended for that. While it might not have been elegant, it was up and workable and the importance of the database was recognized by the researchers who used it. More importantly, it was the only game in town because it represented the only word index available for the *Courier-Post.*

The Dawn of the New Era (with apologies to Arthur C. Clarke)

Over the next few years (into the mid-1990s) the Camden ProCite database did its job in a workmanlike fashion. It wasn't a racehorse, more of a Clydesdale, but it was updated, maintained, and fairly easy to use. Then two important parts of the equation changed: user attitudes and database size.

By the mid-1990s, Rutgers University Libraries made a commitment to provide information access in a Web-based environment.

The reference terminals throughout the library system became Internet-access tools. The catalog, indexes, research guides, and many other resources were all available through the Internet. Rutgers was wired and reflected the nationwide movement of libraries toward electronic access of materials. Students (especially undergraduates), faculty, staff, and other Robeson Library users were now coming to the Library expecting to e-mail, print, or download results.

In contrast to the new, electronic environment, the Camden ProCite database was still accessible from only two workstations in the Robeson Library reference area. It was not networked or Web accessible. Users could not e-mail the results of their searches. Results could be downloaded to disk, but the process was difficult and not at all intuitive.

The Camden ProCite database was growing in size and maintenance needs. Crescenzi, as the history department bibliographer for Robeson Library, continued to do the selection, and library assistant Sandy Marsh continued to input the data. In the mid-1990s, the Rutgers-Camden Public Relations Department donated to Robeson Library a collection of scrapbooks. These scrapbooks dealt with the history of the Rutgers-Camden campus and added a whole new sub-file to the database. As the information in the database grew, so did its use. Assignments for specific courses were constructed around the availability of the information contained in this collection. The situation was reaching a critical point since ProCite was not designed for the type of searching that the users of the product needed to perform.

Technologies that no one had envisioned with the start of a simple clipping file had now become commonplace. Users were frustrated with the perceived difficulty in utilizing the database. The tool had outgrown its technology.

Oh, What a Tangled Web We Weave

The librarians at Robeson Library realized the function of the Camden ProCite database needed to be re-evaluated and that its accessibility had to be restructured. The priorities were established as follows:

1. The Camden database had to be networked and available on the Web.

2. Search results had to be available to e-mail or easily download to disk.

3. The index needed to be able to handle more complex searches.

4. Finally, since the users would have the option to access this database from a remote location, the search process had to be more user-friendly and intuitive, and less instruction-intensive.

The problems facing transferring the database to the Web included:

1. ProCite, the software foundation for the database, is a production tool not a searching tool.

2. ProCite version 1.0 or 2.0 was used in the creation of the database and was therefore too old; there was no direct way to convert the data to Microsoft Access to get it ready for the Web.

3. Users needed/expected to search by keywords. The Camden Procite database utilized Primary Themes based on a controlled vocabulary (subject headings from the Public Affairs Information System Index).

4. Jean Crescenzi had retired and was now a librarian emeritus doing volunteer work with the Camden County

Historical Society. Who was going to assume the labor-intensive task of writing needed abstracts?

5. Discrepancies and lack of standardization for the formatting of the entries resulted in many items being "lost." Entries needed to be "cleaned-up" and standardized. Placement and the use of dates as well as consistency in the use of Primary Themes needed to be addressed.

Ann Scholz-Crane, the electronic information librarian at Robeson Library, assumed the responsibility for the Camden ProCite database. As project manager, her task was to orchestrate the delivery of a user-friendly version of this database to the Web. The actual conversion process was perhaps the most daunting. Fortunately, the Robeson Library had (and to date has) in its employ John Gibson, a gifted undergraduate honors program student and computer ombudsman, who was given the conversion task. First he indexed the ProCite database for its various field delimiters. He then extracted each field—and the information in each field for each record—and converted the information to ASCII text. Next, he relabeled the fields and merged the reformatted information to a Microsoft Access file. Gibson noted that in the conversion process errors are apt to occur, especially in regard to correct size of the field, truncations, etc. As with any conversion some of the data may have gotten lost. But, with the caveat that "clean-up" would have to be done, at last the Camden database existed in a version ready to be put on the Web.

Continuity, accessibility, and standardization are all important considerations when networking. The Robeson Library is part of a library system of roughly 20 Rutgers University Libraries (and growing). Since the Robeson Library is part of a system, the next step was to find a platform to support the database. It would also need links from standard library Web pages to make it available to its primary users, the Rutgers University community. These links would have to be in place for the database to be utilized optimally and seamlessly with the other resources that already existed within the library system.

Scholz-Crane now needed to find an Internet platform to support the Camden database. The computer server at Rutgers-Camden could not handle the direct server access due to the system's security restrictions. She worked on various Web committees with Ronald Jantz, of the Rutgers University Scholarly Communications Center in New Brunswick, and the Camden database project was discussed. Jantz offered to work on the project, install it on the Rutgers Library Systems server, and to set up the search screens. (Jantz's chapter on reuseable platforms in this book discusses at length the technical "how-to's" of this and similar projects with which he has been involved.)

At publication time, the project is at the threshold of being introduced to the public. The prototype database is accessible through the Rutgers Libraries information system on the Internet (http://scc01.rutgers.edu/camden). The database will not be restricted—anyone browsing the Web will be able to access the data. Scholz-Crane is now involved in the lengthy process of standardizing the data: dates, book titles, journal titles, information about the holdings available at Robeson Library, and the use of the Primary Themes.

The actual production of new entries has been vastly simplified by an agreement reached between Robeson Library and the *Courier-Post*, which has given Rutgers-Camden permission to use the lead paragraph of each story (which is copyright protected) selected as the abstract for the database. The keywords of this lead paragraph will be searchable.

The Camden ProCite database is a work in process. One problem still to be addressed is how to make the database more transparent and user-friendly so that a first-time user will be able to access citations with little difficulty. Also, the issue of how to add greater flexibility to the search engine continues to be investigated.

What We Could Have Done Better

When asked to critique the construction of the database, all the principals involved were very forthcoming with suggestions on how to improve the process. Everyone viewed it as a valuable learning experience. Since the database was not originally conceived as a database, and since the Internet was not commonly accessible when the file first began, it is easy to see how the problems of retrofitting an older software package and older technologies to a new environment evolved.

Several common themes run through the suggestions for the production of future databases and for future project planning:

- State the Purpose of the Database as Clearly as Possible—The more clearly you can state your purpose, the easier your other decision-making will be.

- Try to Envision Your Goal as Clearly as Possible—What do you actually want this database to do? It is important to set up short-term as well as long-term goals and to keep them in sight. What will the need for this product be in six months? A year?

- Standardization—While it is impossible to predict with any accuracy what the next electronic search tool innovation will be, it is possible to plan. Using standard templates for the data entry will make the data that much more portable to the next tool that comes along.

- In-House Human Resources—Utilize the talent that resides in-house. Also involve the people who will be the final end-users. They know what they need the product to do and how it should work for them.

- Community Partnerships—The involvement of the *Courier-Post* and the construction of the new item entries greatly simplified the maintenance of the database. When planning the database try to analyze who the shareholders are. Besides the primary user base, who else will be able to benefit from its development and therefore may be called on to share resources?

- Choose Your Software Wisely—When investigating software packages, keep in mind your end-users and the amount of search flexibility that will be needed. Also think about how the results of the searches can be manipulated and how "portable" the data itself will be from package to package.

Conclusions

Few things in life spring full-blown, beautiful, and complete like Athena from the head of Zeus. For most of us mere mortals, the process of creation is a messy one, full of false starts at the beginning and wistful backward glances at the project's completion. Planning, choosing a flexible software tool, and asking lots of questions seem to be a good beginning.

Chapter 3

Women Writers and Online Books

Mary Mark Ockerbloom
Celebration of Women Writers
celebration@pobox.upenn.edu

John Mark Ockerbloom
Van Pelt Library
University of Pennsylvania
ockerblo@pobox.upenn.edu

The On-Line Books Page (http://digital.library.upenn.edu/books) and A Celebration of Women Writers (http://digital.library.upenn. edu/women) are collaboratively developed Web sites with the purpose of making the large number of online books on the World Wide Web more accessible to readers. The On-Line Books Page (maintained by John Mark Ockerbloom) lists complete, published books that can be freely read online. The Celebration of Women Writers site (maintained by Mary Mark Ockerbloom) lists both online books by women and online resources about women authors.

The goal of the On-Line Books Page is to promote the growth of a worldwide, large-scale, freely accessible library of online books. The site seeks to make these books available to as wide and diverse an audience as possible, and help readers find, create, and share books over the Internet.

The Celebration of Women Writers site was created to recognize the contributions of women writers throughout history. Women have written almost every imaginable type of work, including novels, poems, letters, biographies, travel books, religious commentaries, histories, and economic and scientific works. The site's goal is to promote awareness of the breadth and variety of women's writing. All too often, works by women, and resources about women writers, are hard to find. The site provides a comprehensive listing of links to biographical and bibliographical information about women writers as well as books written by women. The site also actively extends those online resources, and has itself published numerous online books by women on the Internet.

Both the On-Line Books Page and the Celebration of Women Writers sites rely heavily on databases. We maintain two related databases, one for books and one for women authors, from which we generate the book and author listings on our sites. In addition to maintaining these databases, we provide background information on related issues, and organize communities to support the growth of online books and author information. For instance, we have written guidelines for transcribing books for online use, and for investigating the copyright status of books. John runs a mailing list, known as Book People, for the discussion of online books and related topics, to which many online book producers subscribe. Mary organizes a group of volunteers, known as the BUILD-A-BOOK project, who collaboratively develop online editions of selected out-of-copyright books by women for the Celebration of Women Writers site.

Project History and Motivation

We began both sites in the early 1990s as personal, spare-time projects, while working in the computer science department at Carnegie Mellon University (CMU). John Ockerbloom was a graduate student when he created Carnegie Mellon's first Web site in 1993, and became the CS department's first Webmaster. He began the On-Line Books Page the same year. (The CS department allows its students, faculty, and staff to use its Web servers for personal, noncommercial projects, but does not directly sponsor or supervise such projects.) When he started the site, a number of early electronic text projects like Gutenberg and Wiretap were putting books online, but readers had to know about each project and search through the individual sites to find particular books. Authors who put up a single book or a small selection of titles were even harder to find. John saw that the linking power of the Web would enable him to create a central directory of online books that could then point to the various Internet sites where the books were actually stored. Such a directory remains valuable even as much larger, general-purpose search engines and directories appear on the Net. In those search engines, links to complete, freely readable online books are often buried under many extraneous hits from secondary references, online booksellers' advertisements, and completely unrelated Web pages that happen to use the same words that are found in a book's title or author's names.

Mary Mark came to the CS department with a background in computers and psychology to work as a research assistant in cognitive science. She started the Celebration of Women Writers site on CMU's servers in 1994, also as a personal volunteer project in her free time.

Mary's initial motivations for creating the Celebration of Women Writers pages were similar to John's motivations for creating his site. Not only was it was time-consuming and difficult to find online books of any sort, but the proportion of online books by women was very small, only about 10 percent of the total number of online books. (Six years later, this has increased to about 18 percent.) Also, since women writers often used pseudonyms, it wasn't always obvious which books were by women. Thus, even when books by women existed and were part of the On-Line Books Page listings, it could be difficult to identify them.

Frustration over the meager online offerings of women writers spurred development of the Celebration of Women Writers site. Given the variety of works by women, it was disheartening at first to find little online besides the works of Jane Austen and the better-known Brontë novels. Were online resources going to recreate a predominantly white male canon of authorship, or might they offer much more? Where were medieval women writers? Children's authors? Poets? Political activists? Scientists? Educators? Travellers? Mystics? Women of color? Women from countries besides England and the U.S.? It was clear that there was a tremendous potential to make lesser-known works readily available to academics and general readers via the Web. Where a print publisher had to worry about the costs of distribution and the viability of small special-interest print runs, an online publisher could create a single online copy that would be widely accessible for little or no cost. Given the increasing interest in women writers over past years, it seemed entirely appropriate to develop a site specializing in women writers that emphasized their diversity and their range of accomplishments. Given the scarcity of resources about many women writers, it also seemed important to include biographical and bibliographical information, in addition to actual books.

From the start, both of us were excited about the potential of the Web to change culture in positive ways. We became strongly committed to making useful and interesting information more accessible. (We also became strongly committed to each other, and married in 1995.)

The On-Line Books Page became one of the most popular parts of the CMU Computer Science (CS) department's Web site. It was one inspiration for the Universal Library project, an official CS department research project that continues to have contact with the On-Line Books Page. John's development of the On-Line Books

Page and his increasing interest in digital libraries influenced his choice of jobs upon completing his Ph.D. In 1999 he accepted a position as Digital Library Architect and Planner at the University of Pennsylvania's Van Pelt Library, combining his computing research with his digital library interests. The On-Line Books Page moved to the University of Pennsylvania with him. It isn't an official university publication, like some of the Library's other Web pages, but John can use the Library's servers for the project, and spend a certain amount of his time working on the pages. The Celebration of Women Writers site is also being hosted by the University of Pennsylvania Library, which has most kindly agreed to provide Web space for it, even though Mary is not employed by the university or the library.

Current Scope

The On-Line Books Page currently lists over 10,000 books that are free and completely readable online. About 18 percent of these are books by women. The Celebration of Women Writers site currently publishes about 120 out-of-copyright books by women, and is developing more editions. In addition to listing online books by women, the Celebration of Women Writers site lists the names of over 8,500 women writers and 3,500 sites about particular women writers, from all countries and time periods. Some of these information sites are local to the Celebration of Women Writers site, but most are found at other locations across the Web.

We get aggregate usage statistics from Web server logs, but do not track individual users. We can therefore only estimate the number of users, but log data collected in February 2000 suggests that the On-Line Books Page is visited about 75,000 times per week, delivering about 200,000 pages of content, while A Celebration of Women Writers is visited about 18,000 times per week, delivering about 40,000 pages of content. We have many volunteers as well as readers. A Celebration of Women Writers' BUILD-A-BOOK project currently lists nearly 300 volunteers on its mailing list, of whom about 50 are actively involved in transcribing texts on a regular basis. The Book People mailing list has over 500 members.

Developing the Databases

After we started our respective sites, the number of listings we maintained grew rapidly. It became clear that the easiest way to maintain our pages would be to store the relevant information in database form, and generate Web pages for the two sites from those databases.

We created two related databases for our listings. One database, used in generating pages for both sites, contains entries for books. Records in this database include titles, authors, and the URLs of free online editions, along with some other cataloging information. The second database, used in generating the Women Writers pages, includes more detailed author entries. Each author can be listed with a variety of names, since women commonly have had different maiden and married names, and often separate pen names as well. Author records can also include dates of birth and death, countries of origin or residence, and a list of URL pages that contain information about the person. (Not all of this information will be available for every author.) To avoid confusion between authors with the same name, we assign a unique identifier to each woman in the author database. This identifier is also used to associate the author entries in the Women Writers database with the book entries in the On-Line Books Page database.

Storing book and author information in database form makes it possible to generate multiple views and subsets of the information. The On-Line Books Page includes browsable listings by author, title, and subject. A Celebration of Women Writers has listings for women authors selected by country and by time period, as well as alphabetical listings by author. If we lack information about one attribute of the author, such as country, the author still appears in the other listings.

Databases also enable searching as well as browsing. On the On-Line Books Page, readers can search for books using information about the author name or title of the books sought, just as they might search a regular library catalog.

We implemented both the databases and their search and generation programs ourselves. John originally wrote the programs in C in 1994, and the present C programs have changed little from the original versions. They run as CGI scripts on an ordinary Unix-based Web server. We also have a few small auxiliary Perl and shell scripts to keep the databases and associated files in order.

We face only minor security issues. We make sure that unexpected input does not make our CGI programs do unexpected things. We also make sure that our underlying database files are not exported via the Web. Although we don't make any money from our databases, we do not want people pirating them and taking the credit for our efforts, since creating and maintaining the databases requires substantial work!

Maintaining the Databases

Much of the value of our Web sites depends on keeping our listings up to date. New books and author resources continue to appear on the Web, and URLs often change, so we need to update our sites regularly to reflect the changing and growing Web. Although we compile and edit the databases ourselves, our readers send us much of the new information we eventually incorporate into our databases, after verifying and checking it against our selection criteria. Each of us has our own maintenance process, similar to the other's but different in some respects.

To update the On-Line Books Page database, John periodically visits the sites of active e-text projects to see what has been added or changed, and to investigate reports of new books and sites (or broken links) e-mailed by readers. He also randomly checks links from time to time.

Mary has four main techniques for updating the Women Writers database. First, she explores published sources for information about women writers, and adds relevant names, dates, and country information to the database. Then she searches the Web for new online information about women writers, and adds new URLs and related information. Third, she responds to e-mail messages from readers suggesting online resources or reporting resources that are no longer available. Finally, since people are more likely to report new links than broken ones, about once a year she runs diagnostic software on the Celebration of Women's Writers pages to detect obsolete links.

Originally, Mary spent a great deal of time gathering information about women writers from published sources to create basic author database entries, and then searched the Web for online resources about those writers. While she still does some of this, e-mail is currently the most frequent source of changes in the listings. Mary probably spends about one week a month searching for new resources in response to readers' e-mail, and updating the database to reflect them. The rest of her time is largely taken up with other aspects of the Women Writers Project, primarily the BUILD-A-BOOK initiative that creates online editions of out-of-copyright works by women.

The main problem we've encountered has been keeping up with the pace at which new books and author sites go on the Web, and with sites that move or disappear. Both in maintaining the databases, and in developing new online resources, we face the challenge of expanding resources while ensuring quality. One way to meet this challenge is to look for ways to automate more of the work involved. Another is to find ways to involve more volunteer help, where it can be effectively used. A third approach is to professionalize some of the tasks involved by creating a legally defined organization with paid employees. At this point, our task is still relatively manageable, and we are concerned most with exploring the first two options. However, we have also considered eventually creating a nonprofit organization, which could be a focus for fundraising and greater expansion.

To date, we have not been particularly happy with the results of automated tasks. While we have made some use of automatic link checkers to find bad links, we found that they tend to turn up high rates of false positives. As a result we have not relied upon them for ongoing maintenance. More often, we will adjust links when we notice on a return visit to a site that the site has been moved or reorganized, or after a user alerts us of a bad link.

We would also like to use automation to more easily incorporate listings for new books and resources by automatically extracting such information from other sources and converting it to our local database formats. Again, the main obstacle we face here is quality control. We would need to make sure that the records we brought in were accurate and appropriate for our site. We have not yet found a way of doing automated or delegated database entry that we're confident would reach our standard of quality. However, it's also clear that we will need more scalable database-update methods in the future, since the number of books online is growing exponentially. Hence, we are likely to continue to explore ways of automating tasks to improve the efficiency of updating the database while still maintaining quality.

We have benefited greatly from the contributions of thousands of volunteers. These include people who formally identify themselves as contributors to the sites, such as the BUILD-A-BOOK volunteers, and others who simply provide useful information or feedback. Someone who e-mails us to report a broken link, or to suggest a new one, may not think of themselves as a volunteer, but they are important contributors. Such informal volunteering is extremely helpful to us in promoting and maintaining the sites.

For promotion, we've relied primarily on word of mouth. We make some low-key attempts to inform people about our sites through related newsgroups, through informing sites when we're linking to them, and through our mailing lists and related projects. Some of our pages are also designed so that they will be likely to come up in book-related search engine queries. Generally we have found that interest in the pages is extremely high. Both the On-Line Books Page and the Celebration of Women Writers sites are widely used. Many sites link to us, and many readers access the Web sites, even with very little promotion on our part. We get lots of e-mail!

Feedback from users is very positive. Our readers appreciate having easy access to resources that would otherwise be difficult to track down and time-consuming to find. Readers are particularly excited when they find some childhood favorite or out-of-print work that they hadn't been able to read in years. Academics have reported that our site makes it possible for them to include materials in their curricula that otherwise would not be available to them. Users are also quite thrilled that the materials we list are available online for free. From the beginning, we considered easy access and free information as crucial features of the sites, and we are committed to maintaining them. We see our mandate as similar to that of a public library, rather than that of a bookstore.

We have also had particularly enthusiastic responses from visually impaired and handicapped people who cannot use or have difficulty accessing other types of resources. Some of our readers view the online books at enlarged magnifications, or put them through text-to-speech synthesizers. Readers who are allergic to paper and ink, or who do not have the motor control to turn the pages of a book, have told us that they use the computer to read the online editions we list.

We had not fully appreciated the importance of online books to such populations when we began these projects, but we have taken it to heart as we develop our sites. Hence, we avoid depending on frames, graphical images, or other design elements in our sites that assume a particular browsing program or interface, instead designing the sites to be accessible to any Web browser. This principle does not require our sites to be drab and colorless. It simply means that we ensure that our information is expressed in a flexible enough manner that all readers can see it. For example, graphical images that are not merely decorative have alternate descriptive text that takes their place in text-based browsers. One advantage of database-driven sites like ours is that it is easy to present the same information in different ways to accommodate different needs, without requiring us to manually maintain separate presentations.

From the start, we have recognized the great collaborative potential of the Web, and have tried to engage others in creating, maintaining, and promoting the resources that our sites encompass. We see this collaboration as crucial to our goals. We are building something that reflects not only our own work, but also the contributions of many others across the Web. Building on shared strengths and resources, we can create something beyond what any of us could do alone. Feedback from readers and Web developers enables us to incorporate information that we might not find without their help. Adding new links to the databases benefits the linked sites and also increases our own worth as a resource. Word of mouth continues to involve new people. Finding better ways to encourage such activities is important. In a digital community, one person can make a difference—and many people, working together, can make a tremendous difference.

One somewhat amusing side effect of the sites' success has been that many readers assume that we receive more direct university sponsorship than we actually have. Some want to know, for instance, if our projects can arrange grants or jobs for them, not realizing that neither project receives direct university funding and that each has operated on a shoestring, or nonexistent, budget. We regard this as a tribute to how much we have been able to accomplish with very little! To date we have not pursued formal grants. It is possible, however, that we may explore this more in the future, perhaps to support new initiatives related to the projects.

Future Expansion

We are interested in extending the pages in a number of ways, and expect the sites and the databases underlying them to continue to evolve. In some ways, the On-Line Books Page and the Celebration of Women Writers sites have each functioned as testbeds to explore particular concerns. Often, we have found it desirable to take some features of each project and apply them to the other project. We're considering a number of changes, including:

1. Extension of search features from the book records of the On-Line Books Pages to the author records of the Celebration of Women Writers pages.

Readers have told us that they would like to search for entries on the Women Writers pages. Search facilities already exist for the On-Line Books database. However, extending search to the authors' database involves more than reusing the existing programs. A women author's search will need to take into account new data fields—alternate names, dates, and country information—that may or may not be available for all entries. This opens up questions about what constitutes a relevant response when only partial information is available. Should someone who is looking for an English author named "Jane Taylor" be given the name of a Jane Taylor with no nationality information, if no other possibility is found? Or should that author record be ignored? If a query asks for writers born between 1800 and 1900, should the search engine return the name of someone whose birth date is not known, but who was known to be publishing in 1835? These are issues that do not arise with the more specific title and author searches we support for online books.

2. Extension of some author information from the author records of the Celebration of Women Writers pages to the On-Line Books Pages.

The date and country information given for authors in the Celebration of Women Writers site would also be useful in the On-line Books listings, for male as well as female authors. Creation of author records for male authors, and association of date and country information with them, would make it possible to search and browse subsets of books and generate small "special collections" according to a reader's particular set of interests. We will likely add such features to the On-Line Books Pages. However, given the much larger number of male authors online, and the huge amount of work required to actually maintain links about writers, it is unlikely that we will try to list online resources about male writers in addition to their published books.

We have also considered what fields we might want to add to book and author records. If both male and female author records are to be created, we may need to enhance basic author records with a gender field to distinguish men and women (unless we simply keep them in separate databases). We might also add fields to identify which names are birth names, which are married names, and which are pen names or other pseudonyms. We have considered adding ethnicity and linguistic information on writers as well, to supplement the existing nationality information. This could allow readers to search specifically for African-American or white writers, for French or English Canadian authors, or for Walloon or Flemish writers in the Netherlands. Similarly, one might extend date information to distinguish specific periods or movements in literature or history, such as the Romantic period in European literature, or the Harlem Renaissance. One might also consider indicating the particular genres in which writers work. At present, however, we have chosen not to try to integrate these types of information into the database, in part because specialized sites often exist that already focus on such groups. These often give much more detailed information than we could readily provide.

In our book records, little attention has been paid so far to the origin of online editions. Recently, we have started to incorporate information on the dates and publications of the sources of online editions for a portion of our entries that clearly draw from one particular print source. However, issues of provenance can be complicated, particularly when the extent to which the online edition replicates the print original is unclear. When an online edition consists of page images, it may often be treated as a facsimile of a specific print edition. Textual transcriptions, however, raise a number of questions. Is publication information about the original text included or omitted? Has the online text been carefully proofread, and to what has it been compared? If changes have been made, what are they, how systematic are they, and are they documented? To what extent does the online edition follow the layout of the original? Does it include illustrations and pictures? Is the entire original edition reproduced, including appendixes, indexes, and advertising, or has some of the front or back matter been omitted? Is the online edition a composite of multiple editions and new commentary? These are some of the questions that complicate the origin of online books.

Potential expansions of our existing databases and Web sites are possible in large part because they were developed modularly. Our database implementation is open-ended, allowing us to easily add new features. Since we implemented it ourselves, we can easily change the implementation to meet our needs as we develop the databases further. The search language, the database layout scheme, and the database vocabulary are all independent of one another, so we can change one of them without affecting the others.

Our somewhat different, though related, purposes suggest to each of us different improvement ideas, which we can then exploit in either project as appropriate.

Nearly seven years after we began our collaboration on the Web, our major goals remain much the same as when we began. We still see the World Wide Web, and whatever may succeed it, as potentially powerful settings for acting in the world, sharing knowledge, and enriching our lives and those of others. We hope that we can help to ensure that people have lots of interesting things to read, and that women writers are not overlooked in this electronic forum. We continue to generate ideas for improvements and new initiatives to help to fulfill these goals. Some ideas may never see the light of day; others may eventually become independent projects. We thoroughly enjoy exploring the possibilities.

Chapter 4

Women and Social Movements in the United States, 1830–1930: A History Web Site

Melissa Doak
Center for the Historical Study of Women and Gender
State University of New York at Binghamton
mdoak@binghamton.edu

Women and Social Movements in the United States, 1830–1930 (http://womhist.binghamton.edu), a Web site produced and maintained at the Center for the Historical Study of Women and Gender at the State University of New York (SUNY) at Binghamton, is intended to introduce students, teachers, and scholars to a rich collection of primary documents related to women's historical participation in social movements in the U.S. Professors Kathryn Kish Sklar and Thomas Dublin co-founded the project in 1997 with minimal expertise and funding. Since then it has grown enormously and now contains more than 300 primary documents, 50 illustrations, and resources and links to other sites on the Web for further research. The site has received national recognition; it was selected to be showcased on EDSITEment as one of the best sites on the Internet for education in the humanities. The rapid growth of the site since its beginning has been exciting, and yet it offers challenges as we struggle to keep pace with its growing size and the plans at the Center for increasing outreach to educators.

The Women and Social Movements site is organized around editorial projects completed by undergraduate and graduate students at SUNY-Binghamton. Each of these editorial projects poses a unique historiographical question and provides a series of documents that addresses the question. In this way each project makes a scholarly contribution to historical knowledge. By the time you're reading this, we expect to have at least 27 projects on the Web site. Undergraduate students in a senior seminar in U.S. women's history completed most of the projects. This course, taught four times since 1997, offers students an opportunity to understand historical research as an interpretive process. Through the development of the editorial projects, students not only become solidly grounded in historical research skills, but also get useful training in the authoring of Web pages.

The site is partially funded by the National Endowment for the Humanities (NEH). Last year, Sklar and Dublin, the project's co-directors, founded the Center for the Historical Study of Women and Gender (which has become the organizational home of the site) as well as outreach efforts for the site and a number of other research projects. I became involved in the project during the summer of 1998 when the co-directors hired me as a graduate assistant. In August 1999 I became a post-doctoral fellow at the Center, continuing my association with the project.

Because Sklar and Dublin conceived of the Women and Social Movements Web site as a resource for teachers at the secondary and college levels, one of our primary goals is to increase the depth and breadth of materials available on U.S. women's history. One of the most exciting things about Internet publishing is its fluidity; the site constantly grows and changes, as do individual editorial projects. Current projects cover such diverse social movements as the female moral reform and abolitionist activism of the antebellum decades, the Woman's Christian Temperance Union, women's suffrage, the women's peace movement, and women's labor struggles in both the New York City Shirtwaist Strike of 1909–1910 and the Lawrence Strike of 1912. By mid-2000, new editorial projects up on the site were expected to include material about the dress reform movement, the Oneida community, the birth control movement, women's anti-lynching campaigns, and the women's rights conventions of the 1850s. We aim to represent diverse women, time periods, and reform movements as we continually enlarge the scope and breadth of the site.

Project History

The project began on a modest scale. Kathryn Sklar conceived the idea in January 1997 when she participated in a panel organized in response to a call from the Library of Congress for the submission of projects for the National Digital Library. While on that panel, she discovered that digitized collections of historical materials about women were scarce. Few women's historians were producing materials for the Web, and none could rival the scale of the larger historical projects already on the Web. She decided to try to remedy that situation and bring more of U.S. women's history to the Web. As a result of dialogue on the panel with participating secondary school teachers, she devised a plan to present primary documents within an interpretive framework that would enable students to learn something about women's history despite the limited classroom time to work with online materials. With this idea in mind, notwithstanding what she felt was her relative lack of technical knowledge, Sklar returned to SUNY-Binghamton determined to fill the need for historical materials about women on the Web.

She got to work immediately. Although the first week of classes for the 1997 spring semester had passed, she presented students in her senior seminar in U.S. women's history with a new research project alternative: They could undertake editorial projects, collect

20 documents that would address a unique historical question, and write a general introduction to the material as well as head-notes and annotations for each document. She also suggested that students who wished to do so could complete their projects in Web site form. By March of that semester, Sklar had recruited the co-director of the project, Thomas Dublin, and had made a successful application to the National Endowment of the Humanities for a small, one-year Humanities Focus Grant. Sklar and Dublin used these funds to hire a graduate student for the 1997–1998 academic year to help create a pilot public Web site.

Michelle Mioff, the newly hired graduate assistant, and Dublin and Sklar worked intensely that fall to mount the first two editorial projects on the Women and Social Movements Web site by December 1997. While they worked with what they considered to be the strongest projects from the previous spring's senior semi-nar, they discovered how labor-intensive it is to transform student work into a reasonably polished project for use by the general pub-lic. Revising and often rewriting introductions and headnotes was typically needed. They commonly rearranged the order of docu-ments and occasionally added new ones where the interpretive argument offered in the original project did not hold up. At other times, they modified the organizing question to one more clearly addressed by the documents at hand. Finally, they had to secure permission to publish the editorial projects on the Web from repositories, publishers, and women's organizations that held rights to the manuscripts or published sources.

Those two original projects, still available on the site, were titled "How Did African-American Women Define Their Citizenship at the Chicago World's Fair in 1893?" and "How Did the National Woman's Party Address the Issue of the Enfranchisement of Black Women, 1919–1924?" Both projects, originally done by students in the spring 1997 senior seminar, and a small related-links page made up the pilot Web site. In spring 1998 Sklar taught the senior seminar again, this time assisted by Mioff, who helped students convert their work from word-processed documents to HTML files. During the summer of 1998, after Sklar and Dublin had edited and revised another group of these student projects, Mioff worked to ready four of the projects for mounting on the growing site. The development of the Women and Social Movements site in its first year helped Sklar and Dublin to obtain a larger, two-year Teaching with Technology grant from the NEH. The new grant funded my hire in August 1998 and permitted the site's more dramatic expansion over the following academic year.

When I joined the project staff as a graduate assistant at the start of the 1998–1999 academic year, the site was in transition; before this it had been a small pilot project, attracting modest numbers of users. My task was to provide the technical support to quickly increase the number of editorial projects available on the site. I had only a minimal amount of experience working on the Web—I had constructed several online course syllabi for professors in the history department and had served as the department's Webmaster for one semester. I was intrigued with the project's mission to place transcriptions of historical documents on the web within an analytical framework that would give students access to primary documents. I believed the project was truly innovative. My growth has paralleled the experience of all of us involved—we have learned from our successes as well as our mistakes as we worked to sustain the growth of the project.

Expansion and Growth

When I began on the Women and Social Movements Web site, my initial task was to transform the undergraduate projects, edited by Sklar and Dublin, into a standard format and then link the projects to the site. At that time the site remained small, allowing just the three of us to handle new projects and maintenance of the site.

We knew little about site design, and because it was still small, we continued to refer to the project as being in the "pilot" stage. However, the site was undergoing a transition. Although only six editorial projects had been mounted in the year and a half since the project began, because the senior seminar had been taught twice, we had about 20 additional projects to choose from as we planned the site's expansion. Sklar and Dublin also recruited several graduate students to create editorial projects based on their own dissertation research. Within a few months we had mounted several more projects and moved the pilot Web site from an instructional server to a server that could be indexed by search engines, essentially making the Women and Social Movements site much more accessible to the public than it had been previously.

Within six months of my hire, it became clear that this project had the potential to grow exponentially. Because of its rapid growth, we increasingly realized that the design of the project had flaws that we needed to address. Our collective lack of experience publishing on the Web made for problems in site design and user accessibility. Although we received much positive feedback about the materials the site made available, we also received some constructive criticism of the site's design. With the help of both an excellent consultant at the computer center and an outside Web developer, we came up with ideas for reworking the site's design as well as navigation around the site. Moreover, my role evolved into a supervisory role as we hired four undergraduate work-study students to do the mounting of new projects, freeing me to address some of the larger problems. In addition to training the undergraduate students in HTML and supervising their work, I also designed and implemented the new format for the site. The new design further standardized the look of the editorial projects, implemented a simple search engine, included better navigational features, and looked much more polished to visitors.

We developed our new organizational scheme with an eye toward making navigation for users relatively easy. Altogether the complete overhaul of the site took more than six months. It still provides the structure for the projects today. From the home page, users can access any of several main pages: a search engine; a permissions page with a list of credits for documents and images; pages providing short biographies and acknowledgments of student editors and staff members; a related-links section; and project notes, which include an editorial practices section. The most important link from this home page leads users to a projects page, which lists the short titles of the projects currently on the site. From there, users can link to short descriptions of the projects and to the projects themselves.

During spring 1999, in addition to our work on the Web site design, we also concentrated on networking with the staff of other Internet projects and informally working with some professors at other universities who began to assign readings from the site in their undergraduate classes. Periodically we requested that one of our undergraduate students spend a few weeks surfing the Internet and writing e-mail to the Webmasters of other academic sites asking them to include a link to our project. In this way we've been able to expand the number of other Web sites from which users were linking to our site, from two in January 1999 to more than 300 at present. Using information collected by the SUNY-Binghamton server, we tracked the increasing number of visits to our site and the growing number of Internet sites that link to our project. During the 1998–1999 academic year more than 27,000 visitors from over 40 countries visited the site, with more than 5,000 accessing it in March alone. By summer 1999, we had completely redesigned the site, our projects now numbered 17, and the site was averaging over 100 hits a day. We were pleased that the average visitor viewed more than 10 Web pages per session, showing that the site was being used intensively as well as casually.

After the period of rapid growth in 1998–1999, our attention shifted in late spring/summer 1999 toward improving the quality rather than the quantity of material offered on the Women and Social Movements site. We assigned one undergraduate to increase the number of links within each editorial project to relevant educational sites elsewhere on the Web. One of my major tasks that summer was to improve the large related-links section of the site as a whole, resulting in the implementation of a three-part links section on the site, including distinct categories of related Web sites: Archives and Webographies in Women's History; Projects in Women's History; and Women and Social Movements Today. We want not only to offer students and teachers a large collection of historical documents within an interpretive framework, but also to direct users to the growing number of other resources elsewhere on the Web for the study of women and gender.

Outreach

My hire as a post-doctoral fellow marked the beginning of another transitional phase for the project. As the Web site continued to grow, we continued to formulate plans for greater outreach efforts. We learned better ways to support the needs of the students who produced these editorial projects in the U.S. Women's History seminar. In fall 1999 Sklar and I team-taught the senior seminar. In preparation, Sklar and Dublin identified several collections of primary documents that the SUNY-Binghamton library owned on microfilm and formulated a set of possible questions about these documents that students could choose to investigate. Students in the seminar selected the topics and collections that most interested them and the questions they wanted to explore. Sklar and I aimed to help the students learn research skills that would allow them to formulate an analytical question and organize an answer through the exploration of primary documents.

A collaborative-learning computer classroom had been completed on the SUNY-Binghamton campus in mid-1999 and we were able to take advantage of its facilities in this third offering of the senior seminar. The classroom contained comfortable wheeled chairs, each with a fold-down desktop arm that can accommodate a laptop computer. Instead of viewing rows of monitors, students viewed one another sitting in chairs in a circle. They worked collaboratively with their peers and individually with us. The equipment and room setup permitted small- or large-group discussions as well as individual work. Laptop computers with wireless Internet connections for each member of the class allowed us to train students thoroughly in the skills they needed to create their Web site projects. The flexible workspace as well as projection technology gave students the opportunity to share their work with others. We developed an extensive course Web site that guided students through basic computer and research skills and HTML tutorials. Students accomplished a great deal during the semester, each of them acquiring a grounding in historical research skills, as well as training in HTML.

The 15 students in the class brought their projects to an unprecedented level of sophistication. At the end of the semester, they proudly displayed their online projects at a reception for invited faculty, librarians, and administrators. The team-teaching approach as well as the technologically advanced classroom enabled us not only to give participants a richer learning experience, but also guided students to produce much more "finished" editorial projects than had been possible in previous seminars.

Future Plans

The dozen excellent editorial projects from the senior seminar waiting to be mounted, the enormous growth of the site, the increasing number of project staff members, and the evolution of several new goals for the site have led us to consider, once again, reorganizing both the Center for the Historical Study of Women and Gender, and the Women and Social Movements site. We now employ five undergraduate students, one graduate student, and one project intern, and are guiding six independent-study students who are working on various aspects of the site. The growth of the staff associated with the project has presented organizational challenges that Sklar and Dublin hope to remedy by obtaining funding for additional graduate assistants who can take responsibility for distinct aspects of the project and for an associate director who can supervise the overall operation and spearhead outreach efforts.

The future of the project, facing the transition necessitated by the site's growing size, rests on obtaining additional funding. The Teaching with Technology grant that Dublin and Sklar secured from the National Endowment for the Humanities has allowed us to construct a site as a resource for high school and college teachers; in the process, the project directors have created a model that we think others can effectively adopt. Sklar and Dublin have now requested a larger grant from the NEH to fund a collaboration with a selected group of college and university teachers. These faculty would develop additional editorial projects and Web sites that would dramatically expand the availability on the Web of quality educational materials related to the history of American women. To prepare for the proposal to the NEH, Dublin and Sklar invited about 60 professors who teach U.S. Women's History at colleges and universities around the country to propose projects for consideration for inclusion in the grant application. Sklar and Dublin then selected 13 faculty at 12 institutions who had demonstrated strong support from their institutions, access to rich archival sources for use with students, and exciting project proposals for possible mounting on their own or our Web site.

This array of scholars from diverse institutions with access to varied and rich archival collections of primary documents will ensure an even broader range of projects. Proposed projects include such topics as women's urban reform efforts in Boston, New York, St. Louis, and Richmond, Virginia; women reformers in the prairie states; women's suffrage in Colorado and Tennessee; women's networks in the New Deal; and political posters from the Women's Liberation Movement. The proposed projects will also significantly lengthen the time span of the Women and Social Movements site, as they range from the antebellum period to the 1970s.

Renewal funding will allow us to help these 13 collaborating faculty members to implement our model on their campuses. We will do this through the development of a manual for the creation of similar Web projects that they and others can follow and through a five-day training seminar for collaborating faculty at SUNY-Binghamton. In addition, prospective NEH funding will permit us to provide support to the selected faculty as they implement their courses and develop their own Web projects.

Even before these collaborating faculty teach their own research seminars, we will encourage them to employ our site as a resource in their own undergraduate women's history courses. We will offer a resource person to respond to their syllabi, propose assignments that make full use of the site's resources, and incorporate suggestions and feedback from faculty as they experiment with the available materials. In addition, we will add to the site substantial pedagogic suggestions for how it might be used more generally in college and high school classrooms. Our goal is to continue to increase the educational value of the site at both the college and secondary school levels.

As faculty are testing classroom uses of Web site materials, we will create a listserv or a threaded discussion on the Web to permit faculty to share their ideas with one another about their teaching strategies. Then the five-day training workshop at SUNY-

Binghamton will prepare collaborating faculty to teach courses in 2001–2002 that resemble our senior seminar in women's history. Faculty will guide their students in the creation of editorial projects using the unique resources available at the different institutions. The following year we will either mount many of their projects on the main Web site or assist those faculty who want to mount the projects on servers at their home institutions, taking care that all projects are accessible to users of the Women and Social Movements site.

Ultimately, we expect that the mounting of projects carried out by the students of collaborating faculty will double the size of our site. We are likely to have about 35 editorial projects mounted on the Web site in mid-2001 when we hold the training workshop. The 12 courses at the campuses of collaborating faculty will probably produce that number of completed projects suitable for mounting on the Web. We anticipate that by the summer of 2003 our site will include or link to some 70 editorial projects with roughly 1,400 primary documents.

Our involvement with faculty at other institutions will not be limited to those selected for intensive collaboration. The project directors are also pursuing funding to work with another 12 faculty who teach the introductory U.S. history survey course, finding ways to support their use of the Women and Social Movements site. Dialogue with these faculty will help us further enhance the educational value of the site. We will also remain in extensive contact with a larger number of college and secondary school teachers who are using the site in their classes. We will encourage contact among these instructors and design a "teachers' corner" on the site to present exemplary assignments and projects that utilize it. We will develop a curriculum for teachers that we'll place in the teachers' corner. Our plan is to greatly expand outreach efforts and encourage increasing numbers of secondary, college, and university teachers to use the resources that the site provides.

We will continue to add editorial projects to the site ourselves. We propose to contribute to the growing diversity of projects on the site by beginning an initiative to develop projects on Title IX of the Education Act of 1972. Title IX banned sex discrimination in schools, in both academic and athletic programs. It has had the greatest impact on athletics, although academic gains for women have been impressive as well in the nearly 30 years since passage of the legislation. We anticipate that including Title IX material will broaden the site's appeal to non-historians. Currently, three undergraduate students are working with us in independent-study courses to ready Title IX material for students who enroll in future senior seminars. We also have begun exploring resources for students who wish to investigate the beginnings of an organized lesbian movement in the U.S. and other topics inadequately addressed by currently mounted projects.

The phenomenal growth of the Women and Social Movements Web site and the various initiatives undertaken by Dublin and Sklar at the Center for the Historical Study of Women and Gender have necessitated a rethinking of the basic organization of the project as a whole. As the site continues to expand, it will contain too many projects for teachers and students to browse effectively. We are seeking funding to create a relational database cataloging system, allowing a much greater level of sophistication in searching capabilities. The database will allow users to browse lists of subjects, titles, authors, and media types; search for specific subjects, titles, authors, and media types; and search for Boolean combinations of subjects, titles, authors, and media types. We also want to increase the quantity of visual materials available on the site, complementing its documentary strengths. The database will allow users to include these graphics in their searches for materials.

The Women and Social Movements Web site, as well as the organization that supports it, is approaching another crucial transition. Concerned that the new technology was bypassing U.S. women's history, Dublin and Sklar began this project on a very modest scale just three years ago, and since then its size and significance have exploded. We believe that the site contributes in a very significant way to the technological revolution taking place in the teaching of the humanities. Our challenges include securing the funding to expand the staff needed for support of the project and to reorganize the site itself in order to accommodate the increasing number and range of materials available on it. Our most pressing challenge, however, is to find new and varied ways to reach out to educators, helping them become producers of online resources, as well as encouraging them to use the exciting new resources available on the Web to teach students about the central importance of women's social activism in American history.

Chapter 5

History Databases at the Library of Virginia

Elizabeth Roderick
Manager, Virginia Digital Library Program
Library of Virginia
eroderick@lva.lib.va.us
http://www.lva.lib.va.us/dlp/index.htm

About the Library of Virginia

Founded in 1823, the Library of Virginia is located in Richmond, the capital of Virginia. It serves as the archival repository for state and local governmental records and as the reference library at the seat of state government. It's also a major research library, with comprehensive collections of materials on Virginia history and culture. There are more than 1.5 million printed volumes in the collection; 58,000 cubic feet of archival records documenting four centuries of Virginia history; 240,000 photographs, prints and engravings; 66,000 maps; and 250,000 reels of archival-quality microfilm. The library has an active publications program featuring a quarterly magazine of popular Virginia history and scholarly studies based on records in the collection.

The Library of Virginia also supports the state's public library system, which serves the population of 6.2 million people through 570 library sites. Services to libraries include consultation on library development and construction, library management, collection development, collection maintenance, technology, professional development and training, and administration of governmental financial aid to local libraries.

The Virginia Library and Information Network

Beginning in 1993, the Library of Virginia initiated the Virginia Library and Information Network (VLIN) to provide Internet access and electronic communications to the state's librarians and library sites. Resources available through the network included access to the Library of Virginia catalogs, printed books and archival resources, e-mail, listservers and newsgroups, bibliographic utilities such as OCLC, subscription search services, and a statewide union catalog and union list of serials.

The Digital Library Program and the Virginia Digital Library Program

By 1994, technological and other advances on the Internet raised questions concerning the future usefulness of VLIN to libraries and their constituents as well as the role of the Library of Virginia in providing computer communications networks. After consulting with Clifford Lynch, a noted library computer applications expert, the Library redirected its efforts toward providing Internet access to its vast collection of unique historical documents, records, finding aids, and photographs. In 1995 it began its Digital Library Program.

In 1998 the Library initiated the Virginia Digital Library Program (VDLP) to provide consulting, funding, and implementation services for local Virginia libraries to digitize and provide access to significant local collections. During Phase I, the VDLP provided the opportunity for 19 local digital library projects at 15 libraries to be developed and completed. These projects included local newspaper indexes, maps, indexes to cemetery interment records, indexes to diaries and journals, ancestor charts, and many local photograph collections.

By the end of 1999, the Digital Library Program had generated digital images of more than 700,000 original document pages; 1,100 maps; 18,000 photographs; and 1.6 million catalog card images. The VDLP had also created 20 new bibliographic databases with more than 300,000 MARC records, 50 electronic card indexes, and two finding aids.

Digital Project Planning Process

Once the organizational commitment was made to the Digital Library Program, staff created a plan and work-flow analysis. Tasks to be accomplished included the identification of potential collections; detailed analyses of those collections; evaluation of preservation issues; documentation of project requirements; estimation of time and costs; analysis of documents; development of indexing strategies; and design of a custom solution for organizing the collections, and for digitizing, searching, and retrieving them. An important element in the development of the digital projects was the requirement that the final products be available over the Internet and that they would not require any proprietary software other than a standard Web browser and viewer.

The Library does not consider the digitization of records in its collections as primarily a document preservation project. We recognize that there are still questions about the permanence of digital storage, and we know that rapidly changing technology may provide improved methods of storing and retrieving digital images in the future. The Library has sought ways to present its collections in formats that will allow flexibility and adaptation to changing technology.

Digital Project Selection Process

At the very beginning of the VDLP, we recognized that the selection process should involve a broad cross-section of Library staff to ensure complete coverage of the institutional knowledge and memory. As a result, the state librarian appointed representatives to a new Network Information Policy Committee (NIPC) in 1995. The NIPC had frequent brainstorming sessions with the staff members most familiar with the Library's treasures. The VDLP staff also turned to the librarians and archivists who worked regularly with the public (and who respond to the more than 20,000 research requests that the Library receives via surface mail and telephone each year) for advice and guidance on suitable collections for digitization. Eventually, a short list of potential projects was compiled.

Selection criteria were developed early and proved to be particularly helpful as the VDLP progressed beyond its initial stages. The criteria were that a project's implementation must be straightforward, with few or no obvious or inherent complications or idiosyncrasies; the materials selected for digitization must be in the public domain or must not be in violation of intellectual property or copyright policies; a project must make a collection or finding aid more accessible to the public; and the project should be a model for similar or expanded implementations.

Preserving "Labors of Love"

Many of the fully searchable databases and other electronic indexes for many significant collections produced by the VDLP represent the salvage and preservation of the "labors of love" of both paid staff and volunteers over a span of more than 100 years. The indexes to these significant collections exist in many formats, ranging from fragile index card files to handwritten/typed lists and charts, word-processing files, and databases compiled using a variety of software products including Leading Edge, Microsoft Works, Microsoft Word, Microsoft Access, dBASE, Excel/Lotus, FileExpress, Paradox, etc. The VDLP, working with the vendor, developed customized procedures to handle and translate the data contained in these formats to the standard MARC format.

Conversion to MARC Records

The data is initially converted from its original format to ASCII. This takes a level of complexity out of the process—there is no need to maintain the presentation of the data (columns, boldface, underlining, etc.), but the challenge is to normalize the data without losing any content. Then the data is pre-processed to make the conversion procedure easier and more accurate by converting to mixed case, removing extraneous punctuation, adding required punctuation, and setting database indicators correctly. The data is then reformatted into columns for review via a Web-based interface prior to full conversion. Then a program is written to convert the data to MARC, which involves parsing the ASCII data to isolate specific data elements such as author, title, date, etc., then moving data elements into their appropriate MARC tags/subfields, according to specifications. Finally, the most essential and time-consuming step is quality control. VDLP staff analyze the resulting MARC records for accuracy. Some problems can be detected and corrected programmatically, some problems can be detected programmatically and corrected manually, and some problems can only be detected and corrected manually.

One of the most critical processes for any digital library project is careful analysis of the materials to develop a file-naming scheme. The file name assigned to each individual image is used in many ways, and it is very difficult to redo this step. The file name is how the image is identified in the directory structure of the image server—it is entered into the MARC 856 field to provide a link between the bibliographic record and the online image, and it is used later by our photographic services staff when retrieving the archival master from the CD-ROM to make copies for customers. The decision-making process for the file-naming scheme can take several weeks and will be frequently revised as we discover anomalies and inconsistencies in number schemes. Very little other VDLP activity can proceed until this process is complete.

Resources Required to Implement and Maintain Projects

Personnel Resources

The Library does not have much flexibility with adding staff when new programs are initiated. At the beginning of the Program, only two full-time staff members were available to work on the new projects. The Library solved this problem by expanding an already-existing relationship with our library automation vendor, VTLS, Inc., to include large-scale digitization and database-creation projects. VTLS, being a private corporation, had the flexibility to hire additional staff as needed to work on projects. They had at their disposal a universe of available part-time staff at Virginia Tech, located in Blacksburg, Virginia. Members of National Honor Societies at local high schools were also hired to work on the projects. During Phase I, the VDLP also recruited volunteers from other Library of Virginia organizational units to help with many tasks and made use of the Library's emerging formal volunteer program. As the VDLP grew, additional full-time and part-time staff were added. The Program now employs four full-time staff and up to eight unclassified part-time staff who work full-time hours. All VDLP staff must have the ability to do the following: perform repetitive tasks over long periods, handle fragile and rare materials, analyze documents and images for detailed content and to express that content via the cataloging process, learn new skills and technologies quickly (and preferably have an interest in the content of the materials), and work with staff in other Library organizational units. VTLS has expanded its imaging department to accommodate the additional needs of the Program.

The overriding consideration that determines who will work on a particular project is whether or not we can remove the materials in the collection from the Library for processing. The Program staff handles those that we cannot remove, and the vendor handles those that we can remove.

Maintenance Issues and Error Reporting

Ongoing maintenance involves the staff of the Library's information technology (IT) department, which maintains the server that houses the integrated library system software, the databases, and the Web gateway software. System backups, upgrades, and restoration procedures occur regularly. The VDLP staff is responsible for maintaining databases or for transferring responsibility for maintenance to other Library organizational units. If transferred, Program staff provides all necessary orientation, training, and ongoing support. The servers housing the images and other software applications require care and feeding, including space and resource allocation, directory and file structure maintenance, backups and upgrades, and off-site storage of data.

The VDLP has implemented an Error Reporting System, making it possible for online users to provide information to Program and vendor staff about errors and problems discovered within the resources. Previously, various staff members would field e-mail reports and questions from users. As the number of resources continued to grow, it was essential to streamline and formalize customer service to ensure that there was no confusion about who was responsible for fixing an error, that efforts were not duplicated, and that e-mail was not lost or overlooked. It was also necessary to provide instant status updates on all errors, to ensure more timely responses to errors reported by users, and to maintain an ongoing record/history of the problem-resolution process.

We created a form on the server that prompts users for the following information:

Requestor Name:

E-mail Address:

Name of Database: (A pull-down menu lists all possibilities)

Type of Browser:

Browser Version:

URL: (For example, http://eagle.vsla.edu/cgi-bin/drip.gateway?
                authority= 0024-95180&conf= 010000)

Error Location: (A pull-down menu lists all possibilities, such as Database Record, Image of Electronic Index Card, Text of Index Points that Link to Groups of Electronic Cards, Photograph Image, Map Image, Intermediate Screen Link to Document Image, Collection Description, Search Tips, Help Screens, Other)

Text of Error Report:

Error Message:

Additional Info:

After the user submits the form, it is stored with other reports in the Error Control Menu. The program manager reviews this menu regularly, and after reviewing a report decides to assign the error. Each staff member reviews the menu daily for assignments, and assumes responsibility for researching and correcting the error and replying to the user about the status of the error. Once an error is fixed, staff members attach a reply to the error report, send an e-mail to the user that the error has been fixed, and update the status to "R—replied to." If there was no e-mail address or a reply seems unnecessary, the status is changed to "D—done." If staff members cannot fix the error themselves, they attach a reply with their notes and change the initials for the report to the person who needs to review it next. Everyone can view all of the correspondence for errors, and we always know exactly who is working on them and why.

Technology Resources

The Virginia Digital Library Program resources reside on three UNIX servers. The digital images and several key software applications are located on two of the servers, and the Library's main integrated library system software is located on the third server. The bibliographic databases created by the Program reside on this third server, along with the Web HTML gateway software that links the database records with the digital images on the other servers. These servers require UNIX system administration resources, thus requiring Program staff to be proficient with the UNIX operating system and UNIX text editors.

Program staff must also be proficient with the MARC format; standard library cataloging and classification processes and procedures; cataloging software; the characteristics of digital images, including image formats; scanning equipment including flatbed and high-speed scanners, digital cameras, microfilm scanners, transparency scanners, CD-ROM capture equipment, and traditional photographic print processing; and image-manipulation software such as Adobe PhotoShop.

The interface to the Library's bibliographic databases is a fully functional, MARC-record "Webcat." The Web gateway software makes the Library's online catalogs and other resources available to any Internet patron who has a Web browser that supports HTML 3.0 tables. The gateway runs on industry-standard UNIX servers using PERL (Practical Extraction and Report Language) and HTTPD Web server with CGI (Client Gateway Interface) support. The online catalogs can be searched by author, subject, title, call number, and general keyword; or by a user-defined search. The gateway offers three different levels of catalog searching: basic, advanced, and expert. An advanced search allows for Boolean, or word combination, searches. An expert search allows for search expressions and word combinations.

The Web gateway was tailored to the Library's specifications for each bibliographic database, including the names and types of searches; stop-words used in title searches; names of screens; button style and button labels; language strings used for screen headers, footers, and error messages; and help screens. The design and functionality of the bibliographic databases are consistent from collection to collection. Collection descriptions and customized search tips are provided for each database, as are context-specific help screens for every database screen display. In those databases where available, the digitized images are linked to each database record via the 856 field and retrieved by clicking on a multimedia icon.

In one case, the VDLP was forced to delay the release of a digitized collection of more than 900 large-scale maps until the technology to display the maps efficiently and effectively over the Internet became available. The Program chose not to undertake the development of an expensive custom solution, which turned out to be the right decision as a company by the name of LizardTech (a successful spinoff from Los Alamos National Laboratory) developed a raster-image compression software product called MrSID (Multi-Resolution Seamless Image Database). This relatively inexpensive product makes it possible for multiple resolutions to be generated from one image file and viewed across the Internet in seconds. No browser plug-in is necessary. The software permits browsing of an image of any size (pan, zoom, and explore it), while the image quality maintains its sharpness, and its selective decompression lets users access any portion of an image as quickly and easily as another.

Standards

The Virginia Digital Library Program creates bibliographic records that adhere to all national and international standards, in part to ensure that these records can be contributed to all appropriate national and regional bibliographic utilities and union catalogs.

The Library is creating digital masters of all images at the highest appropriate resolution for each type of media, for offline and off-site storage, to ensure that all significant information contained in the source documents is fully represented. However, we scale the digital masters to reduce the displayed image size in a way that balances image detail against image size and that addresses resolution, compression, bit depth, image orientation, and image format. Other factors we consider are the aspect-ratio of the image and the aspect-ratio of the screen, and the need to scale, without sacrificing legibility, to achieve the complete display of images while reducing excessive scrolling by the user.

Marketing/Public Relations

The Library of Virginia uses a variety of avenues to market existing and new digital resources. The Library operates several Internet listservs, including two that deal with Virginia history and Virginia genealogy. This is a primary target audience, so announcements of new resources are sent to all subscribers of these lists. Announcements are also sent to a number of other listservs, including DIGLIB, IMAGELIB, various H-net (History Network) lists, LITA-L, etc. The Library publishes a bimonthly newsletter, and new resources are described there. Announcements are submitted to other appropriate print publications. Program staff are often asked to submit articles to print and electronic publications, and they regularly provide live demonstrations to a variety of groups, internally and at professional organization conferences. Occasionally, local and statewide media outlets will feature a new resource. Organizations and individuals who maintain Web sites will often feature the VDLP and provide a link to it. We also submit site information to the available services that will distribute it en masse to popular search sites.

Realizing that most of our new users will discover the resources as a result of performing searches using Internet search engines, we are diligent in including all relevant metatags (metadata) to the main pages for each resource. This data is positioned within the <HEAD></HEAD> tags. The following metatags are most often used by search engines for indexing purposes: <META NAME="Keywords" CONTENT="keyword1, keyword2, keyword3, etc.">

Usage Statistics: How We Use This Data

The Library collects extensive and detailed usage and statistical information about all the VDLP products through the use of readily available server-analysis software. The transactions recorded include:

- Total transfers by request date (bytes sent by date)

- Total transfers by request hour (bytes sent by hour)

- Total transfers by client domain (indicates the country of origin, and the type of domain: .org, .mil, .com, etc.)

- Total transfers by reversed subdomain

- Total transfers by URL/archive section

- Number of hits on the main DLP portal page

- Number of hits on each product home page

- Number of hits on all help screens

- Number of document, map, and photograph images viewed (for each digital collection)

- Number of searches performed in each bibliographic database by type of search (basic, expert, advanced)

The information is used extensively and in a variety of ways. We use statistics to determine which resources are popular and which are not. This data drives future projects or new iterations of existing projects (such as reformatting or expanding). The data also tells us the level of use by geographical location (by country) and when the resources are most heavily used, both by time of day and day of the week, which helps to determine server and database maintenance downtimes. Finally, by communicating the scale of VDLP use to the staff and vendors working on the various projects, we can enhance morale and enthusiasm for what is often tedious work. The data can be used to demonstrate that the expenditure of funds was appropriate and that continued funding is desirable.

Security Issues

Each server is protected from outside damage through the use of firewalls, file ownership and permissions, passwords, etc. Incremental backups are performed nightly and full backups weekly, with the security tapes held off-site. However, the overriding concern for Library staff is that by making these resources widely available over the Internet, we are relinquishing our intellectual ownership and control over the materials, and that a user will download a document or image and republish those materials without obtaining permission or paying usage fees. Although not yet implemented, the staff continues to research digital watermarks, digital object identifiers, and other encryption techniques to identify the images as the property of the Library.

Impact on Users

The worldwide dissemination of databases, finding aids, and images of original library and archival materials provides many benefits to researchers. Intellectually, it provides access to online resources that are available 24 hours a day and available for use instantaneously, access to online resources that the user might not know existed, and provides the opportunity for repeated use and accessibility over long periods. It also eliminates the need for users to be selective in what they choose to examine or request for delivery, and facilitates the stimulation of research ideas by access to a broad body of material. It also allows for the possibility of serendipity, or the discovery of one online resource while pursuing another. The speed of the research process can be enhanced through instant access to original documents, photographs, and maps. This will affect the time required for a researcher to develop ideas and theses from research notes to published document, and the time between a researcher's initiating research and any monetary return expected from this research. It will also potentially eliminate the time (and cost) spent via traditional means (mail or fax) to provide identical documents to more than one person for review and comment so that geographically dispersed researchers can examine an online document simultaneously. Ideally, this will facilitate discussion and speed the procurement of answers to questions or help in the removal of research impediments.

There is a difference in readability between the original document, a microfilmed image and the digital image. Visually impaired researchers who have difficulty reading microfilm and original documents can benefit from access to high-quality online images. The user also can manipulate the digital images of original documents through magnification, zoom, and cropping.

Furthermore, the distance between the user and the Library is eliminated. Handicapped individuals, senior citizens, or those who cannot afford to travel, but who have access to the Internet, can use many of the Library's materials. A researcher can then more accurately assess the cost/benefit of traveling to the Library to view the original documents in person. The online availability of research materials will also reduce the repeated handling of fragile original documents, thus preserving them for use by those who must absolutely examine the originals.

Some disadvantages include the inability of users to afford adequate computer equipment and high-speed Internet connections, the requirement that the user employ left/right and up/down scrolling to view a document on the screen, and the subsequent fragmentation and difficulty in comprehension.

Impact on Internal/External Relationships

By providing the opportunity for anyone in the world to learn about the Library's holdings, we increased the demands placed on staff members working in different departments. For example, the number of interlibrary loan (ILL) requests and orders for copies of documents or photographs increased. Many staff members were uneasy about learning new technologies or approaching their work flow in different ways. Plus, in using the online resources, we also increased the demand for personal customer support. And the physical traffic to the Library has grown because of the increasing availability of finding aids and document images online.

Cost/Benefit Analysis

Although the initial cost of creating digital images and associated indexes, databases, and finding aids can be high, the online presentation offers greater opportunities for distributed uses, with a subsequent lower unit cost per use. By traditional means, library users incur costs to travel to the Library of Virginia to examine original materials or to request paper copies of them remotely. Some of these costs, for travelers from other states, include long-distance telephone calls placed before the trip, babysitters or house-sitters, automobile travel or public transportation, lodging, meals, and charges associated with photocopying and other on-site research work. Hidden costs include the value of vacation leave from a place of employment; the cost of lost research hours, as the Library is not open in the evenings or on Sunday; and the cost of time spent searching indexes, finding aids, and library catalogs before identifying, evaluating, and copying relevant documents. The Library also incurs costs to provide this information, which include the salaries of personnel needed to help patrons in identifying needed documents.

The costs for a user who requests materials via surface mail are less obvious, but can include service fees charged to out-of-state users, limits on the number of research requests that they can request at one time, a long turnaround between the time we receive a request and the time it is processed by Library staff (because of the thousands of research requests received by mail, the surface-mail user ordinarily must wait an average of 6 weeks), limits on the number of microfilm reels that we can send via one ILL transaction, etc. The potential delays may also affect research or publication deadlines. Plus, there is the cost associated with pursuing a line of inquiry whether or not a relevant document exists. Perhaps the requested search will prove fruitless, in which case the service fee for staff time expended is nevertheless charged to the user. Those requesting copies remotely also involve Library personnel to process requests, retrieve documents, prepare the copies, complete billing and accounting procedures, and mail the materials.

Through the use of time-and-motion studies, we can track the costs associated for these traditional transactions. By identifying the hourly cost for each staff member involved in the transaction (salaries + benefits + FICA + other costs), then breaking this down into a per-minute cost and counting the number of minutes each staff member spends on that transaction, we can then estimate the cost for each person involved in the transaction. By totaling all these, it's possible to estimate a total cost per transaction.

Capturing detailed cost information for each project enables us to determine the development cost for one database record or one digital image. Over time, we will be able to determine the proportional reduction in cost to the Library to serve the online patron, and to compare these reductions to the costs associated with serving the on-site and surface-mail user. The development cost of the database records and digital images, per transaction, will be offset over time.

Pitfalls and Solutions

The toughest challenge we faced was a logistical one, involving cross-institutional staff coordination and a division of responsibilities. By uniting everyone behind a common goal and then developing and documenting a detailed action and team interdependence plan, we were able to get a tremendous amount of support from all groups. Besides the technical and team coordination challenges, throughout the Program we had to deal with a variety of issues ranging from investigations into the provenance and copyright of material to safely handling fragile, rare, and sensitive materials.

Since the Library of Virginia does not view digitization as a preservation alternative, a policy was initiated soon into the VDLP that we would digitize no library materials if they had not first been microfilmed. One of the earliest projects was digitizing the Family Bible Records collection, which we had never filmed. We scanned each page image using a flatbed scanner but, in hindsight, we should have microfilmed the collection first. We neglected to consider how much time quality control would consume during and after project completion. We also neglected to consider how much time staff would spend providing assistance to users via e-mail and telephone.

For our photograph projects, we initially rephotographed each image and created a slide. These were used to create PhotoCDs, which were used to load images on the server. We now use digital cameras or flatbed scanners, which eliminate several steps in the process and reduce costs. A constant problem is managing the sizes of the image files, and finding a balance between image quality and the time it takes to download images over Internet connections.

We maintain very detailed unit cost information for each project. This makes it possible to adjust the workflow to increase efficiency, project costs for future projects, and perform cost/benefit analyses over time. At the beginning of the Program, we could not have anticipated the impact increased availability would have on other departments such as interlibrary loan, photographic services, and public services.

Communication among Library staff and with our vendor is complicated so we created a listserv to make it easier. All e-mail messages and replies are seen by everyone, and all of the messages are archived in a fully-searchable Web-accessible database.

Throughout the life of the VDLP, we have had to assess our situations constantly, identify problems and opportunities quickly, and be prepared to take advantage of our existing and anticipated resources. The Program has helped us understand better the critical linkage and balance between change, tradition, innovation, people, and technology.

Chapter 6

Taking a Database to the Web: A Case Study

Vicky H. Speck
Editorial Director, Serials
ABC-CLIO
vspeck@abc-clio.com
http://serials.abc-clio.com

Introduction

All database publishers, whether university libraries, associations, or commercial houses, face the same questions when deciding to take a database or a collection to the Web. Is this a database or collection suitable for Web delivery? Why is a Web product desirable? What are the costs and how will they be covered? Is there sufficient technical and editorial expertise in-house to do the work, or are outside resources needed? How much time will the development process take? What ongoing support will be needed once the database or collection is on the Web?

Almost three years ago, ABC-CLIO, publisher of *Historical Abstracts* and *America: History and Life*, started exploring these issues in developing the Web versions of these two history research databases. Both are highly respected abstracting and indexing research tools used for academic research in history and the other social sciences. Web versions were finally launched in September 1998, almost two years after the Web-development process started. *Historical Abstracts* covers the history of the world outside of the

U.S. and Canada from 1450 to the present. *America: History and Life* covers the history of the U.S. and Canada from prehistory to the present. Between the two databases, there are over 1 million entries.

Parts of the underlying data had been in one electronic format or another for a number of years. The databases have been included on DIALOG since 1975, and CD-ROM versions of the databases have been available since 1992. Entries from the 1950s and early 1960s were available only in print form.

Why Take a Database or Collection to the Web?

Web delivery of reference information is almost a given nowadays. Library users expect access to information when they want it, where they want it, and in a format that is convenient for them. Consequently, librarians are demanding that reference publishers provide Web versions of products so that patrons can have access 24 hours a day, seven days a week without having to go to the library in person. If commercial publishers wish to maintain a product's economic viability, they have to meet or exceed these customer expectations.

There's a perception in the marketplace that Web technology is the way that all, or at least most, information will be delivered and that if the information is not on the Web, it is not available at all. Most librarians have anecdotal information about students refusing to look at print reference resources, even though they may be quicker to use and more accurate. The generation of students now in elementary schools is even more focused on the Web as the way to find out anything.

The CD-ROM version of the ABC-CLIO databases was developed with a DOS interface in the early 1990s. The DOS format was very stable and compatible with a number of university computer systems, but customers had been requesting a Windows-based interface for a number of years. In addition, the CD-ROM platform selected has good data and index compression tools that allow large amounts of data on one disc. By the late mid-1990s, Windows had become the predominant operating system in many academic institutions, and library patrons had grown accustomed to using a mouse rather than arrow keys to navigate around a screen. Libraries were getting rid of CD-ROM towers whenever possible, as computer systems were upgraded to accommodate Web technology. The decision to make *Historical Abstracts* and *America: History and Life* available on the Web gave ABC-CLIO an opportunity not only to address customers' requests on the product format but also to revamp the interface and the underlying search engine to make it look and function in a more contemporary fashion.

Some publishers decide to make a Web version of a collection available because they have received special funding or a special mandate from a university or scholarly society to do so. Others make the decision in order to realize new opportunities for subscription revenue. Still others make the decision because a key player within the organization has the drive to develop a Web version of the product and will do whatever is necessary to make the event happen, including the bulk of the work.

Creating the Development Team

Every publisher taking a product to the Web faces the question of resources, whether it hires an outside developer or does the job in-house. The development of Web projects can be just the technical challenge that many systems people love. Whether the staff has the necessary expertise or will have to learn while doing the job is a consideration. Also, can the staff take on this challenge and still do the work that they were originally hired to do?

Whether a publisher uses in-house staff or hires an outside developer to do the work, there are associated costs. With an outside developer, there is the check that must be written monthly or at the end of the project—and those checks can be substantial. With in-house staff, there is the routine systems work that still has to get done while development is taking place; additional hires may be needed to supply crucial programming skills.

A hard decision to make is whether the in-house staff has the expertise—and interest to do the project. It can be costly if the staff does not have the needed experience and goes down several dead-ends before coming up with a working solution. A publisher would have gotten the project done more quickly and at a lower cost by going to an established development house.

At ABC-CLIO, we employed a hybrid approach, using in-house staff in conjunction with an outside development group after looking at the option of sending the whole project to a commercial database developer. We decided to not turn the project over to a developer for several reasons: (1) the costs, (2) the concern that the data would be forced into a predetermined format that might not suit the data, and (3) the need for future independence from an outside developer. ABC-CLIO is also fortunate to have seasoned in-house CD-ROM development and production staff, part of our information technologies group. Their assignment was to support the electronic versions of the serials, which at that time included only the DIALOG and the CD-ROM versions. They understood in detail the file structure of the data as it came out of the internal production system and had developed the filter applications to format the data for the existing electronic delivery. They also had significant technical support experience with the CD-ROM versions of the databases, which provided them insight into every aspect of how customers use electronic reference material, from software support to research results. They did not have specific Web-development experience but were eager to learn. We joined this group with a Santa Barbara-based Web-development group and added editorial, marketing, and library expertise from within ABC-CLIO to form the Web-development team.

The Process—or, We've Got the Team, What's Next?

The very first thing the development team must do is talk about the vision of the final product—its look and feel. Our first step was to sit down with the representatives from the outside development group and discuss the possibilities and pitfalls of the Web. We learned at the outset, when designing the interface, to be aware of bandwidth limitations for the customer. Next, we used the successful CD-ROM interface as a template to design a no-nonsense Web interface. We also had discussions about the fields that researchers used most frequently (which were critical and superfluous), the criticisms of the existing CD-ROM interface, and the information that most researchers want displayed when they received their results set.

This discussion ranged over several meetings until we were in general agreement about what we wanted. The Web-development group then collaborated to produce a complete site proposal, including user interface, search functionality, and customer content. This proposal was prepared in a series of storyboards for the site. The storyboards outlined what the opening screen would look like; the look of the various search and display screens; and the general look of FAQ screens, help screens, and output options screens. We then handed the proposal to the outside development group. Some publishers might wonder why we didn't bring the developers in immediately, but the ABC-CLIO Web-development team already had a clear picture of how we wanted the site to function. We didn't necessarily know how to make it work, but we knew what we wanted the final result to be. We needed to make sure that this vision was communicated as clearly as possible to the outside development group, who had no prior exposure or understanding of academic research databases. We had several reviews of the storyboards to make sure that the desired result was crystal clear. This process served us well; when the outside development group's interface development fell short of our expectations, our group took over the responsibility for all the HTML interface coding and graphics.

At this point, the product remained close to the original proposal, with the notable exception of the use of frames, which had been part of the early storyboards.

Making the Data Electronic

There are two aspects of creating an electronic database or collection. One is the functionality or the engine used to retrieve the data, the other is the form or interface that the user utilizes to access the data. The data used in the creation of the print and CD-ROM versions of the databases are already available electronically in a fielded flat-file format, and even though filter applications had to be rewritten to accommodate the Web application, it was not a formidable task. The greater problem was the fact that the first 18 years of Historical Abstracts were available only in print, and we had to create usable electronic files. After looking at several alternatives, we decided that the most cost-effective solution was to send the 18 volumes of entries overseas for re-keyboarding but to re-key the index portion of the earlier volumes in-house. We also used in-house production and editorial staff to add elements to the earlier entries so they would contain data similar to current entries. It took us three years to complete the project; volumes 1 through 5 of *Historical Abstracts* became available electronically in December 1999.

Alpha, Beta, Gamma—Or, You Can Never Get Too Much Feedback

One of the lessons we learned early on was that "smaller is better," at least as far as development datasets are concerned. All of the early phases of development were done with the equivalent of one volume's worth of data per database rather than the full set of data. Such small datasets allowed for quick database builds when new programming was added—without having to wait the hours that it took for the full database to recompile.

Prior to beta, we had to abandon several features and redesign some functionality, including the initial search engine, frames that would allow controls to float in view, and a dictionary-style browsable index. The initial beta was very different from the proposal. We were open to some experimentation in the process, including the use of a commercial browser search engine recommended by the outside development group to augment the custom engine they were developing. We built a prototype database using that engine and invited a group of local academic librarians as well as in-house editorial staff to review the prototype. There were a few things they hated and a few things they loved. The group generally liked the look of the interface, but they did not like the search engine nor the existing version of the browsable index. The overall feedback was that we were on the right track. What they really appreciated was the fact that we included them early in the process so that they could provide effective feedback on what the final product looked like and how it functioned. We used the feedback from these sessions to overhaul many key features and completely redesign others (such as the browsable index).

We were still adding and refining features to the site. One of the things we learned quickly was the lure of "feature-itis." People on product development teams frequently want to add features to the product to enhance it and make it more attractive to users and customers. At some point, these features become costly in terms of time, money, and complexity, and the development group must determine whether a feature is worth the cost to produce it.

The next step was to refine the Web application suite, which went relatively fast. As we identified and fixed bugs or "search anomalies," we started including ever-larger datasets whenever the databases were rebuilt. The gradual inclusion of larger datasets helped us find out how long it would take to build the entire database as well as whether there might be any speed problems associated with the search engine having to go through a greater number of records to locate the pertinent ones. It was at this point that we learned that the natural language time period functionality wouldn't work, and we began to adapt the time period functionality of the CD-ROM engine. A unique feature of the ABC-CLIO databases is the ability to limit a search by time period, and we knew users expected this feature and that it had to be intuitive.

Meanwhile, we were recruiting librarians at academic institutions across the U.S. and Canada to act as beta testers. We officially went into the beta phase of database development in May 1998. Over the next several months, the librarians provided us with valuable information concerning retrieval speed, the accuracy of the information retrieved, and other desired features, as well as the whole look and feel of the database screens. The user interface went through several revisions. Doing all this work in-house reduced costs and produced the best result. Even today, we still get feedback and questions e-mailed to the Web tech team and the Web content team. At several locations throughout the databases, e-mail links pop up at the click of a mouse to allow users to send messages to either of these groups. Both groups take these messages seriously and respond to users' questions and comments in a timely manner.

Fun Stuff Along the Way

As we worked on this database development project, we kept coming up with ideas that would make the whole search process easier for the user. One of the early goals was to limit the need to scroll throughout the site. We decided that the search screen would take up no more space than what was available on one screen on a optimally sized monitor (e.g., Netscape Navigator and Microsoft Internet Explorer versions 3.0 and 4.0, with a screen size of 800 x

600). We suspected that most searchers would not enter data in more than three fields before hitting the "search" button, so we wanted to make sure that users would not have to do extensive scrolling to fill in the appropriate search fields. This required that certain underlying data fields be consolidated, which necessitated changes to existing data filter applications. This assumption was validated later when we reviewed isolated search records and watched users enter searches at product demos at conferences. It also created a lively internal discussion as to where the search button should be located. The ultimate decision was to locate a long, narrow "search" button along most of the right-hand side of the search screen. This button allows the user to enter search terms into the appropriate fields and drag the mouse immediately to the right to initiate the search without having to go to either the top or the bottom of the screen. The limitations of current technology still prevent the use of the "Enter" key to initiate the search.

One other feature we included was an optional search progress window that allows the user to see how many records are identified for each element of the search. That way if a user feels the search is taking too long, the search can be terminated and then modified to exclude those elements that are taking a significant time to search. This tool is good for tracking the progress of long or complex searches and also is an invaluable troubleshooting tool.

One of our databases' output options is one that allows users to e-mail the records to themselves or to others. (This feature is becoming fairly standard in most reference databases.)

If readers wish to see some of these features in action, they can search demo versions of our databases at http://serials.abc-clio.com. A click on the "Sample Database" button will bring up a demo version of either *Historical Abstracts* or *America: History and Life.* The datasets underlying each of the demos are one volume of data.

Even with a stable Web product, the development team meets on a regular basis to plan new features and enhancements to the product.

Problems Along the Way

In developing Web versions of *Historical Abstracts* and *America: History and Life,* we had decided that there were two functions we really wanted: natural language date searching and browsable indexes in several fields. We weren't sure the technology was there to support the functions, but we wanted to see if we could make them work. Eventually, we had to revert to an earlier version of time-period searching rather than natural language searching. We did get a usable version of the browsable index, even though it isn't what we ultimately want for the product.

For any type of history database, being able to search on a time period field is crucial. The dataset a user retrieves using "war" as a keyword with "1860" as the pertinent time period is different from the dataset the user retrieves using the same keyword with "1914" as the time period. It is possible to search using more focused key-words, but history research is frequently built around specific time periods, so an easy method of time period searching is an absolute must. The CD-ROM versions of these databases use a series of decades and centuries entries. The user opens up a browsable index and selects a time period. This time period is then automatically added to the search screen. The development team hoped that with the power of the Web we could let users just enter the desired dates, say "1914–1917," and the search would select the appropriate entries. The designers developed the functionality, and it tested beautifully with smaller datasets, but we discovered as we added more data to the database that the functionality slowed down tremendously—it was taking minutes instead of seconds to do sim-ple searches. Users were not happy with this development, and we had to substitute the method of time period searching used on the CD-ROM for the natural language date searching. We've not given up on natural language date searching, but it is currently not a high priority. We hope that changes in technology will give us a boost in that direction in the near future.

Browsable indexes created another challenge. Browsable indexes are important for certain fields in a database, because frequently a controlled vocabulary is used and the user may not be able to immediately identify what terms a particular database publisher uses without browsing through the appropriate index. In addition, there may be certain fields like "journal title" that have a number of similar but not identical names that will produce different results based on the entry selected. On the CD-ROM versions of the databases, they were accessible by arrowing down to the appropriate field and hitting the F2 key. The index opened up and the user could use type-ahead navigation to locate and select the appropriate terms to be entered in the search. We knew the only way that the identical functionality could work on the Web was to first download the entire index before the user selected the pertinent entries. With several of the fields this would be easy to do, but with others (such as "subject terms," our key controlled vocabulary index) this would present a major problem. The number of entries in that list is such that it would take as long as a half-hour to download before the user could do anything—we knew that nobody would wait for that to happen. We also knew that all browsable indexes had to behave in an identical fashion. After much trial and error, our in-house developers devised a method that would download segments of the index as the user called for them. The functionality, which includes index searchability, works well and is consistent, even though it is not as seamless as we would like. This is still an area we are trying to improve.

FAQs, Help Files, and Other Things

As we completed the programming for the project and were in beta testing, we knew that we would have to start writing all the supporting documentation that the site required. The elements that needed to be written included any prompts that appeared on screen, a FAQ for the database, and help files. We decided to include in the FAQ all the elements of a more technical or general nature. We generated a list of appropriate questions, and then ABC-CLIO's editorial and technical staffs composed answers that were reviewed several times before they were posted. We continue to add questions and responses as issues or changes to the databases arise.

The help files focused on the specific data fields within the database and would include an explanation of the field and as many examples as possible. Much of the work on the help files was done by editorial staff members and was based on real questions asked by the beta site users. After several months, we changed the help file programming to allow for context-sensitive help files in addition to the larger help file itself. This means that the user can view the help file explaining a particular field by clicking on the underlined field name. It puts the help information right at the user's fingertips.

24/7: Who's Responsible?

Users expect Web information to be available 24 hours a day, seven days a week, 365 days a year. They want minimum downtime for maintenance or other delivery problems. This demand places a great burden on information providers. Do they host the databases themselves or do they put their trust in an outside hosting service? If they choose someone outside, how do they select someone reliable?

One of the considerations driving the decision is a concern about computer security. Anytime that someone can enter a system, there is the potential for a security breach and data destruction. Firewalls provide some measure of security, but sophisticated hackers have been known to break through them. Having separate computer systems, one that outsiders access and one for internal systems, is an option. Another option is a hosting service with a reliable backup that can replace any damaged data should hacking occur.

Other considerations include the ability to invest in appropriate equipment, such as storage devices and processors, and the bandwidth to support the expected access to the databases. On-call staffing to cover outages is another need that must be addressed.

Some criteria used to evaluate suppliers of hosting services include:

1. Reliability

2. Reputation

3. Level of service

4. Ability to support the language the program is written in

5. Capacity (both servers and bandwidth)

6. Ability to act quickly in response to problems

It is always a good idea to check references. Most hosting services are happy to supply names of satisfied customers for potential customers to contact. In addition, there needs to be a system of accurate and immediate notification if the host site goes down. It is an embarrassment to get a call from a customer telling you that your site is down when you know nothing about it. We developed effective notification procedures and established who receives the notice from the outside vendor and who notifies our customer service staff. We also developed a separate Web site, our Web status page, that is located on a separate device from the databases. Customers can access this site to find out whether there are problems with the database site. If the site goes down, our policy is to post as much information as possible about when the site will be available again. Any expected downtime is scheduled to provide the least inconvenience to customers as possible, and those expected downtimes are posted on both the Web status page and the databases themselves as soon as possible.

To minimize the user impact of adding new information to the databases, our development team devised programming to build new datasets in the background and then quickly substitute the new dataset for the old one. We also keep a backup set available in case there are problems.

Hurray, It's Done! Or Is It?

The immediacy of the Web is both a blessing and a curse. Use of Web technology brings with it the expectation that what you are receiving is the most recent information. For an information provider, it means that you are constantly adding more data and improvements to the site. It's no longer possible to sit back and wait for things to happen. As soon as the site is up and running, you're already beginning to design the next version of the site.

The impact of Web delivery is much broader than just the Web site itself. Since we brought up *Historical Abstracts* and *America: History and Life* on the Web just over a year ago, we have made several minor revisions of the site, we are completing work on a major revision, and we have changed editorial and production system procedures to provide more data on a monthly rather than quarterly basis. Doing things the way they've always been done is no longer an option, and a publisher has to accept those challenges if it wants to be a player on the Web.

Summary—Helpful Hints

Our development team learned a host of lessons while working on this project. Some of the lessons are summarized below.

1. It will take more time and frequently more money to complete the project, and the parts of the project that one assumes will be the easiest to do frequently are not.

2. The tool or utility that one is sure must be available to do some of the work usually does not yet exist. Everyone agrees

it's a great idea, but the tool must be created before the project can go any further.

3. "Feature-itis" can be costly and can complicate the vision of what the publisher is trying to accomplish with the product.

4. Hardware problems can cause just as much trouble as software problems. At times, one must troubleshoot to find the real cause of the current problem. The hardware problem may be on the user's site and not necessarily on the host site, but troubleshooting must be done at both locations.

5. Never underestimate storage space or processing power. A good estimate is to double what you expect to need. (We've had to upgrade hardware twice since our databases were made available on the Web.)

Web delivery of information, particularly reference information, is where much publishing effort is being directed, whether it is publishers such as ABC-CLIO mounting its own products on the Web or companies such as netLibrary mounting electronic versions of reference books from a number of publishers. To do it well requires time, attention to detail, and a vision of what an electronic version of a print product could look like and how it could function.

Chapter 7

Road to Papermoon

Brian-John Riggs
Papermoon Books
papermoonbooks@earthlink.net
http://www.abebooks.com/home/BJJR

I moved to the town of Gibbsboro, New Jersey, during the fall of 1999. I didn't know many people there so I would often take week-end bike rides to get acclimated to the area. One afternoon I spotted a small sign on a wooden post that read "Book Barn." The sign hung on a corner among several Victorian-style houses, but I did-n't see any sign of a bookstore. I turned the corner and there it was: a big red barn. So I hopped off my bike and decided to take a look. I entered the store and was absolutely amazed: a converted barn wonderfully decorated in old, out-of-print books. The walls were lined with shelves, and there were chairs set about for readers to spend quality time with their interests. I fell in love with the place and would visit it as often as I could. I even purchased a 12-volume set entitled *The Works of Benjamin Franklin*, printed in 1904.

I've always been an admirer of out-of-print books and was elated that my new town provided me with a place to further my hobby. The following spring I took a friend to the Book Barn to show her my secret treasure. As we approached the door I noticed a sign on the door that read: "No longer open to the public." I was devas-tated. Below those terrible words were, "You can now find us at www.abebooks.com." I still wasn't satisfied. I turned the doorknob and it was open. A young man sat behind a computer with a large box of books to the right of him. I inquired about the transition, and a gentleman appeared from behind one of the shelves. He said: "We're completely online now. Seventy-five percent of my business was coming from the Internet, so I decided to lower my overhead and put the entire business online." I was a little confused and a little sad. What he said made sense, but I felt like a part of my whole bookstore experience was dying.

Some time had passed and my heart was mending so I decided to dig up Book Barn's Web address and check it out. I logged on, but there was no sign of the Book Barn. Again, I was confused. I finally found abebooks.com and figured out exactly what was going on.

The Enlightenment

The home page for abebooks.com is extremely informative, and it didn't take me long to figure out what the company was about. Advanced Book Exchange (ABE) is located in Victoria, B.C., and is the largest of the online book-matching services. The site combines booksellers from the U.S. and Canada into one database. The unique part about ABE, as well as the participating booksellers, is that they deal exclusively with out-of-print books. The best part about the database is that a person can search for a book by title or by author and then visit bookstores throughout the country. Of course, they'll only be visiting the stores via the Web, but it's still a genuine experience.

I was interested in checking out abebooks.com, so after entering some basic information I was logged in and allowed to explore. I entered the "Search" area and a very basic form appeared. I found that once I entered the details of a book, the database searches for every bookstore that carries it and lists them individually. Descriptions and logistics about the book are given along with the individual bookseller. It also gives you the option to go directly to the bookseller's Web page. For the next month or so I continued to search through the database at various intervals and began to use my own books as search tools.

I've been collecting books for several years. My collection primarily consists of out-of-print books and old college textbooks. Over the past few years, I got into the habit of stopping in old bookstores and yard sales and picking up whatever looked good. My collection eventually outgrew my bookshelves and I was forced to store new acquisitions in boxes. This practice ultimately converted my spare bedroom into a storage facility. I continued to use my own books for searches because they were easy tools and I wanted to see how other booksellers valued their books. After comparing prices from bookstores around the country I found that I was able to pick up a few treasures over the years. At that point, I knew I was somehow closer to opening my own bookstore. I decided that I would look into what it would take to become an online bookseller.

The Dream

The thought of becoming a bookseller always interested me. I envisioned myself in a dark little store on some main street in New England. My bookstore would be lined with old books and I would sit all day and attempt to write a novel while a young college student minded my store. This was my goal, and my target date was somewhere between 10 and 15 years away. However, as I continued to ponder the online scenario my vision began to change. Instead of a little shop in Maine, my shop would be my study. Instead of paying someone to handle customers, my computer would virtually work for me. I would be my own boss and my shop would never close.

The first step I took to becoming a vendor was learning how to categorize my books. During my previous searches on abebooks.com I noticed that all of the books listed had peculiar descriptions to them—almost like a secret code for the serious collector. This was a bit intimidating at first but with a little patience and a little research I was able to graduate to a level of understanding. There's an icon on the abebooks.com home page entitled "glossary," and that helped me decipher the various descriptions. Up until this point the process was relatively painless. I spent another couple of weeks looking through the glossary and performing searches. I began to get very comfortable with the various terms and realized how much I didn't know about out-of-print books. Abebooks.com made it very easy to download the glossary, and I refer to it as often as I can. My desire to start my own site grew and I ventured closer to becoming a part of the abebooks.com family.

The abebooks.com home page lists several options for everyone who visits it. The options are self-explanatory and very basic, and I clicked on "learn how to join our bookseller network." I was instructed to first create an inventory of my books. There are several programs available that are geared toward inventorying books, but abebooks.com provides a free download of one that I have found to be extremely user-friendly. The program is called Homebase2 and I highly recommend it to anyone interested in becoming a bookseller.

I spent, and still spend, an enormous amount of time loading my inventory. It's a tedious process, but there are several advantages to Homebase2. One advantage is that it allows you to work off-line—this is essential because the inventorying process is time-consuming. At first Homebase2 intimidated me. I began to waver on whether or not I was ready to become a bookseller, but the more I worked with my books the more interested and determined I became. My determination began to spill over into my personal life, which ultimately became very beneficial for me. My family and friends surprised me by donating boxes of old books. There were even instances when friends of friends donated books. Before I knew it, my storage room was becoming full and my soon-to-be inventory was expanding. My study, which would eventually become my store, was evolving but I was still a long way from opening shop. I would spend hours at my desk, loading books into my database.

One advantage of all this quiet time is that I really got to learn about the books I was inventorying. During loading I began to notice authors from similar time periods. I learned about regional publishers and the types of books they published. I learned about first editions and how to classify the conditions of my books. It was also during my loading period that I was reminded of the Book Barn. I remembered the guy sitting behind the computer, a book to his right, probably a copy of the glossary to his left, and hours of loading ahead of him.

Another advantage of Homebase2 is that it forces a bookseller to organize his inventory. This was particularly helpful for me because I'm naturally a scatterbrain. Once a loading session is completed there is an option to upload the updated inventory to the abebooks.com account. The two work in conjunction with each other and uploading is extremely easy. It took me a little while to set up a vendor account, so I kept my inventory in Homebase2 until I was ready to commit.

Finally, I decided that my dream of owning a bookstore could become a reality. At this point several things crossed my mind. I wasn't sure if I was going to be able to devote the time to setting up a virtual business. Another concern was whether or not I was going to be able to afford it.

I decided not to rush into anything so I broke the process down into several steps. My first step was, of course, entering my inventory into the database. Once I became somewhat efficient at logging in my books I would have more time to work on other aspects of my project. I wanted to be thorough, so I read everything I could on the abebooks.com home page. I visited local bookstores and asked the owners if they had heard of it. I read as much as I could about the program from every available source and spent a lot of time calling the support line. I found that the responses I received were positive. The support team at abebooks.com was extremely helpful, and although I wasn't able to find extensive literature on the company, what I did find was very encouraging.

The next step I took was signing up at the site to become a vendor. This process was relatively easy, and I was pleased at the set-up cost. Abebooks.com charges a $20 monthly fee to become a vendor, and a $40 initial fee that goes toward the first month's payment. I found this to be very reasonable considering the amount of services provided. Part of the process is the actual setting up of the account. In doing so, abebooks.com transferred all of the information I used while searching the database and converted it into a new vendor database. Before I realized it, I was an actual vendor and my interest in developing my bookstore grew stronger. Logging books was no longer tedious but worthwhile. I informed everyone I knew that I was opening an online bookstore and—besides the occasional "you mean like Amazon?"—my support network grew. Then another realization struck. Not only did I have all of my inventory stuck on my computer, but I still didn't have a Web site.

Fortunately, abebooks.com provides each vendor with a free Web page along with the tools to customize it. I spent an evening customizing my Web page and was satisfied with the results. Upon the completion of my new site, abebooks.com launched it immediately. This was very helpful in motivating me because I now had something tangible—something that I could look at and tell other people to look at. The Web page provided allows each vendor to display general information, such as phone and fax number, address, and e-mail, as well as general descriptions of what the bookseller offers. It is also possible to search either the bookseller's inventory or abebooks.com's inventory from my Web page. I often checked my page two and three times a day just to see if I was still in business. It quantified and qualified me as a bookstore owner. My elation over almost opening shop was short-lived. I realized that in order to generate any business I had to upload my inventory. This was a very scary time for me, and it took a long time to complete it.

I was very tentative in uploading my books because I still wasn't 100 percent confident in my ability to classify books. By this I mean that I didn't want to describe a book a certain way, and because of lack of practice, sell someone something that wasn't exactly the way it was supposed to be. There are specific terms used to describe the books (i.e., condition, binding, edition) that must be accurately applied. As the bookseller, the responsibility lies within myself. I was entering an arena that was, for me,uncharted territory. Not only was I no longer a casual collector, but now I was a dealer in out-of-print books selling exclusively through the Internet.

One of my major concerns was with transactions. I work full time for a small company and I know how difficult arranging payments can be. I was worried about how I would bill customers and how customers would pay me. At first I thought that I would just ship everything C.O.D. and deal with payments that way, but I didn't think that would be very professional. Then, shortly after I was up and running, abebooks.com introduced Abe.Commerce, which handles the sale of all books from beginning to end. I'm now responsible only for delivery and maintaining my pledge that the book I send is the book I described. This was an enormous relief for me because it solidified any doubts that I had about my new venture. I could now operate my own bookstore efficiently and completely at my leisure.

Since I've joined abebooks.com they've introduced another option for vendors. 21 North Main (http://www.21northmain.com), which is a database that offers abebooks.com services to university and college libraries throughout the country, is the company's latest effort to allow many more users the opportunity to take advantage of its services. By uploading inventory to 21northmain.com, librarians can find books that they otherwise may not have access to.

As soon as I became a vendor through the abebooks.com database an update came to me in the mail. Basically, abebooks.com wanted me to expect immediate activity and suggested that I be as prepared as possible. At first I thought it was a sales pitch but the following evening I came home to find an interesting e-mail. The message was from a gentleman who had come across my Web page and wanted to know if I carried a few books that he was interested in. I was elated. Results. I couldn't believe that in a single day my Web site, without my complete inventory posted, could generate an inquiry. It read:

> *Dear Antiquarian Book Dealer:*
>
> *A search of your home page indicates you may have copies of the R.R. Donnelly Lakeside Classics. If you do find the books listed below will you please let me know of their availability. Also, kindly keep my list on file.*
>
> *Thank you.*

My reply read:

> *Dear Mr. Moore:*
>
> *Thank you for showing interest in my bookstore. I apologize for not having my inventory available for you to search, but I am currently in the process of uploading it. I do not have the books that you inquired about but I will keep my eye out. I was very excited to receive your mail because you were my first visitor. I have just launched my site and that is why my inventory is not complete. Once again, thank you for visiting Papermoon Books and please keep in touch. I have added you to my customer list, and I*

*will update you if I come across anything that I
think you might be interested in.*

*Sincerely,
Brian-John Riggs*

Shortly thereafter, the gentlemen replied:

Dear Brian-John:

*You have my best wishes for every success in your
bookstore venture. Do you have a particular area of
interest? Please keep in touch.*

I was sad to tell him that I wasn't able to fulfill his request, but
maybe one day he'll be my first customer, too. Either way it was a
rewarding experience for me.

I often find myself wondering whether or not it was too easy. I
wonder if I missed a step somewhere, and maybe I didn't cross all
of my t's and dot everything that should have been dotted. As of
now, everything is okay and I do my best to keep up on updates provided by abebooks.com.

The reasons I became an online bookseller are many. For one,
I wanted to interact with others who shared my interest. I find it
peaceful to browse in bookstores and chat with people who frequent them. Now, instead of browsing, I'll be interacting with
them via the Internet. I'll be in contact with people all over the
world and possibly become friends with people that I otherwise
would never have met. I also wanted to do something with my
books. I don't anticipate making a million bucks with my bookstore, but I really don't mind. If I can sell a book that was of particular interest to me then that's payment enough. The other reason I started my online bookstore was because I wanted to be
active on the Internet. I wanted to participate in what is happen-
ing now and my bookstore is a constant teacher.

Chapter 8

21 North Main, Inc.

Jeff Strandberg
21 North Main, Inc.
jstrandberg@21northmain.com
http://www.21northmain.com

Background

It was tailor-made for an Internet solution: used, rare, and out-of-print books available for sale by the millions, sought by libraries but scattered in holdings of thousands of used-book dealers. A fragmented market of upward of 16,000 sellers and only half as many institutional buyers, responsible for one-third of the estimated $2 billion yearly demand for used books. Yet much of their demand went unmet because the desired titles simply could not be located.

The fragmented nature of supply made acquisitions of used and out-of-print books by libraries a time-consuming, costly, and inefficient process. Searching to fill accumulated "want" lists of up to 5,000 volumes, buyers foraged for used and out-of-print books using every conceivable method of communication, from phone to fax and e-mail to simple word of mouth. Despite their almost universal connectivity to the Internet, and their routine use of it for book purchases and collection development, librarians and acquisitions technicians were unable to locate 60 to 85 percent of books sought. And while a well-developed direct-distribution chain connects the publishers of new books to buyers through booksellers, that chain is broken the moment a retail sale is made. The 1.4 million books now in print are but a tiny fraction of those ever published, yet most are now available only on the used-book market, if at all.

Until now, technology had established little more than a narrow beachhead in the used-book market. Nearly 40 percent of used-book dealers have an online presence, but less than five percent of their inventory is available online. Needless to say, the challenge of locating specific books for library acquisition in such an environment can be daunting.

Enter 21 North Main, Inc., an emerging Internet company in Minneapolis-St. Paul that launched http://www.21northmain.com in spring 2000. 21 North Main was built around the simple idea of consolidating books from a vast network of independent used-book dealers into one Web site, with functionality and features tailored especially to meet library needs.

Pre-Launch Insights

The dictum that says, "If you build it, they will come" may have been true in a popular baseball movie, but in e-commerce it is sheer folly. Just one glimpse at any list of top searches on Web engines ought to be convincing proof of the necessity of detailed research on market potential and characteristics as a precursor to any business-to-business (B2B) or consumer-oriented Internet venture.

An early market assessment conducted externally by graduate business school students yielded important information, and many key findings were subsequently corroborated by 21 North Main's own detailed proprietary research—a useful and economical approach for start-ups.

Software-development expenses tend to dominate the financial landscapes of all emerging Internet companies, and 21 North Main proved to be no exception. Whether in-house talent or outside consultants, technical expertise is a costly imperative, necessary for building the proprietary systems and software design that provide competitive advantage and serve as barriers to entry for potential competitors.

Develop a solid business plan to serve as a combination roadmap and Bible early in any Internet enterprise. It is essential in obtaining investment capital in the crucial incubation period when operating income is nonexistent, but development costs significant. The "solution-in-search-of-a-problem" pitfall materializes whenever the real motivation behind launching a dot-com enterprise is simply to join the e-commerce revolution. A prudent business plan can minimize the risk of letting seasoned business judgment succumb to temptation.

A Strategic Alliance

Developing strategic alliances and marketing partnerships with established operations on the Web is an excellent way to ensure that a start-up e-commerce venture offers the most state-of-the-art, comprehensive product or service possible. On the eve of its launch, 21 North Main bolstered its own online database of used and out-of-print books by entering into a joint operating agreement with Advanced Book Exchange (ABE). Located in Victoria, B.C., ABE is the largest of the online book-matching services, facilitating the sale of some 10,500 used, rare, and out-of-print books per day. This made it possible for 21 North Main to offer libraries:

- The largest online inventory, with over 15 million used and out-of-print books available online

- Some 4,500 used-book dealers united in a single network database, with the option to continue preferential arrangements with designated dealers

- Competent, responsive, and knowledgeable specialists for locating books not available online

Most book dealers participating in 21 North Main's program upload current inventory holdings using a software package called Homebase2 that is provided free by ABE to its dealer network. These frequent uploads serve to refresh the database with newly added titles and remove ones that are sold or in pending orders. From an information systems perspective, one of the major benefits of the ABE/21 North Main alliance was the creation of redundant, mirror site computer systems in Minneapolis-St. Paul and Victoria. By making remote site hosting possible in the event of catastrophe, the alliance also had valuable benefits for disaster recovery, safeguarding the chief intangible assets of 21 North Main and ABE—reliable Web sites available for e-commerce 24 hours a day, seven days a week.

Integrating the complex, dynamic flow of information about order status and fulfillment, constant changes in the inventory holdings of thousands of dealers, and customer queries and responses between 21 North Main, ABE, dealers, and libraries is a challenge. The division of labor is described in the task list that follows:

    Dealers

        Registration

        Uploads

        Q & A's

        Fulfillment

        Payment Received

        Wants

        Shipping

    ABE

        Dealer Registration

        Inventory Acquisition

        Order Fulfillment

        Payment to Dealers

        Q & A's

        Matching (wants)

Shipping

Book Return

21 North Main

Business Development

Marketing

Order Submission

Cancel Order

Get Vendor Profile

Vendor Search

Customer Service

Payment to ABE (List of Books)

Wants

Preferred Dealer Capture (Transfer Info to ABE Through Customer Service)

Libraries

Registration

Book Search

Book Bag

Book Detail

Q & A's

Preferred Dealers

Payment to 21 North Main

Wants

Order Submission

Order Display

Order History

A Peek Behind the e-Curtain

The innovation that allowed libraries to select books seamlessly from millions of titles held by thousands of separate dealer inventories in constant flux, hold them in electronic baskets for consideration later, or consolidate purchases by credit card or purchase order demanded a substantial effort in programming and design. Behind 21 North Main's Web site, extensive software customization was required.

Information had to flow continuously in real time across the North American continent. Data integrity and ordering information had to be safeguarded. Data uploads from dealers required dynamic integration into the database to keep it up-to-date. Books pending for purchase had to be flagged electronically to hold them in suspense from other users. The intricate maze of applicable taxes, tariffs, and customs duties that loomed the moment foreign customers executed orders, coupled with shipping costs for overseas delivery and local levies imposed on foreign dealers by host governments, dictated that 21 North Main temporarily limit sales to only within the U.S. at launch. And finally, a customer's ability to upload "wants"—titles desired but not located in online inventory—had to be channeled to the appropriate dealers who specialize in a particular genre.

At 21northmain.com, Web users submit and request information—the lifeblood of e-commerce—for processing in Platinum, a database management system leased by 21 North Main. Platinum enables 21 North Main employees to perform front-and back-office functions on customer service, accounting, and marketing that either cannot be automated or require personal intervention, assuring responsiveness to customer requests and rapid order fulfillment. Data flows between the strategic partners, customers, and dealers. Internal users (developers, customer service, marketing, finance, and other areas) exchange data with suppliers (dealers, libraries and other institutions, individuals, and estate sales), buyers (dealers, libraries and other institutions, and individuals) with external users (ABE, and two companies that provide computer and Internet services). Books flow between buyers and suppliers. It is essential for buyers and sellers to be able to communicate by e-mail directly with one another as well as with customer service at 21 North Main.

The wisdom of experience suggests that even the best-designed information system structured around state-of-the-art technology may take longer to implement, and often exceeds budgeted expenses. But launching a complex Web site prematurely, with an assortment of stopgap patches and hardware not meeting specifications, may lead to unanticipated problems later. Testing that is limited to the closed environment of a network cannot possibly simulate the potential higher levels of user activity or transient conditions on the Internet. 21 North Main's launch was announced to the market in segments to ensure that customer service could respond quickly and not become overwhelmed with requests for assistance.

First-time visitors to any Web site will not linger for long at the site if it's plagued by repeated system crashes, or down altogether. Repeat visits to such a site are usually nonexistent, especially in cases where a customer resorts to contacting the provider of the malfunctioning Web site by e-mail or telephone and fails to receive satisfactory customer service or, worse yet, no response at all.

A Virtual Marketplace

21 North Main embodies what the investment firm Bear Stearns calls a "metamediary," a B2B enterprise that augments an established but inefficient distribution system with the efficiencies of Internet-based e-commerce, surrounding product delivery through that new channel with value-added services and expertise.

Instead of disrupting established channels—and risking alienating book dealers and library customers in the process—21 North Main serves as a market clearinghouse, maintaining no actual physical inventory. Orders are forwarded to dealers and books shipped directly from dealers to buyers. In contrast to matching services offered by online used-book exchanges, 21 North Main has developed an advanced e-commerce model that blends the largest online inventory of used and out-of-print books and the efficient functionality of online purchasing and consolidated billing. As a metamediary serving both sides of the market—supply and demand—21 North Main has expanded selling opportunities for dealers while delivering greater efficiency and service to libraries.

The essential component of this exchange model is a "virtual" marketplace—an e-commerce Web site—where sellers may display their wares for inspection and purchase by buyers. The concept is as old as commerce itself, but it took the widespread advent of Internet access by fragmented independent booksellers before it became applicable to the used and out-of-print book market.

This virtual marketplace concept is what distinguishes 21 North Main's e-commerce model from that of others. 21 North Main provides the mechanism for efficient trade between buyers (individual bibliophiles and institutional collectors) and sellers (used-book dealers). 21 North Main neither acquires nor carries an inventory itself, focusing instead on building brand identity and loyalty to attract buyers and sellers, and facilitating a secure means for con ducting financial transactions.

21 North Main's marketplace offers users and used-book dealers in the network all the essentials of efficient commerce:

- The largest online catalog of some 15 million used, rare, and out-of-print book titles, with descriptions and data on the location, condition, price, and relevant terms

- A search engine that automatically matches inventories with titles sought

- An e-commerce function supporting online buying and efficient order entry with dealers

Research indicates that less than five percent of all used books have been cataloged electronically. If needed books aren't found via an immediate database search, 21 North Main opens access to this inventory by broadcasting buyer want lists directly to the dealer network. Through this unique device, 21 North Main will make the combined physical inventory of all participating dealers available to buyers.

Visitors to 21northmain.com are guided to a user-friendly search engine that will allow buyers to enter a few simple search parameters, such as author and title, or to enter complete want lists. In contrast to many popular consumer Web sites—where screen after screen is cluttered with distracting banners—the prime goals of 21 North Main's Web screen design were to achieve logical appearance, navigability, and ease of use.

For instance, the engine will search the inventory database, make matches, and advise the buyer of available materials. If the book or books are not found, the search request will be retained and the database will be searched once every 24 hours until all books are located. When matches are made via these automated searches, buyers will be notified of the available items via automated e-mail.

What makes the 21 North Main model so unusual is its e-commerce function. When books are located, shoppers may make a purchase through a simple credit-card transaction (institutional buyers are able to execute orders via wire transfers or rapid processing of e-mail invoices). When purchases are made, 21 North Main will order the books from dealers for direct shipment. No other online used-book service currently offers this feature.

21 North Main's goal is to become a used-book marketplace rather than an online bookstore. The distinction is critical. Amazon.com, the archetype of the online bookstore, acquires

inventory of all books it offers and sells. Well known eBay and other high-profile e-commerce ventures operate without inventories, but lack focus on a single market or product.

By contrast, 21 North Main, which is focused on a single product category and a single discrete market, carries no inventory and handles no products. Instead, it simply provides the mechanism for efficient trade between buyers and sellers. Overhead is limited in comparison to traditional brick-and-mortar operations. Recognition of revenue from e-commerce enabled 21 North Main to accelerate growth using cash flow from operations instead of external capital to a degree not possible in most start-up ventures.

Expertise or distinct competence in delivering a product or service is vital for sustaining a commercial Web endeavor. It provides competitive advantage through differentiation, opens niche markets, and reinforces customer loyalty. It would not have been enough for 21 North Main simply to offer a "virtual marketplace" without also connecting the unfilled "wants lists" submitted by libraries with the large percentage of used-book dealer inventory holdings available for sale but not accessible online.

Marketing Tidbits

An e-commerce Web site designed for libraries must be marketed differently than one targeted at for-profit corporations, and especially compared to one catering to consumers. A marketing strategy designed to move potential customers from awareness to interest, interest to desire, and desire to action (e.g., purchase or use) of a new product or service offered on the Internet must first pierce the clutter inherent in the Web. With an almost unlimited trove of information, the World Wide Web resembles an enormous library, except that it lacks the structure in classifying, cataloging, organizing, and locating information that users of libraries enjoy.

It's difficult to imagine a marketing campaign to reach potential users that strives to leave impressions of a long, inscrutable URL character string. It would be akin to a book publisher promoting what is hoped to be a new bestseller by that book's assigned Library of Congress call number. 21 North Main's initial marketing campaign consisted of a distinctive four-part direct mailing to key decision makers in libraries that coincided with Web site launch. It was designed to create awareness of the new company and its offering, to reinforce that awareness in weekly increments, and to stimulate users to try 21northmain.com.

Monitoring Web site traffic by the number of "unique visitors" is not the vital indicator of success of a marketing program in B2B e-commerce that it is on the consumer side, where there may be no other way to gauge the effectiveness of a media campaign.

In addition to direct mail, another avenue was chosen to reach the desired audience without having to cut through the clutter of the Web. 21 North Main became the exclusive sponsor of Garrison Keillor's *Writer's Almanac* on National Public Radio, a twice-daily program that reaches millions of listeners. It is economical, reaches a large audience of potential buyers, and always includes mention of 21 North Main's financial commitment to volunteer literacy programs.

Why would an Internet-based company bypass the Internet as an advertising delivery medium? Because its target audience was relatively compact, well defined, and readily identifiable, making it ideally suited for direct mail, reinforced by public radio.

Final Observations

Becoming the premier Web site for libraries interested in locating and acquiring used and out-of-print books required that 21

North Main provide access to the largest possible database of books, accessible via a customized search engine with sophisticated e-commerce capabilities.

Launching a Web site with only the most rudimentary features and attempting to incorporate enhancements later while the site was active would have been disruptive at best, and possibly disastrous. A reliable, fully functional e-commerce Web site available to users from the outset entails greater effort and expense, but it is worthwhile in the long run. An emerging Internet company's reputation relies heavily upon the image provided through a simple URL link.

What advice can be offered to others contemplating creating or developing an e-commerce site? First and foremost, gain as much knowledge as much as possible about the intended market—its size, characteristics, buying behaviors, and competitive forces, to name only a few variables. Develop reliable sources of market intelligence, not only from potential customers, but also from sources that are widely available but often overlooked.

Never rush to market for the sheer sake of being there. Although information moves at lightning speed on the Internet, the race for business on it is a marathon and not a sprint. Test an effective prototype thoroughly before allowing general access to it—repeat visits are unlikely from users who visited a half-baked Web site, only to leave it frustrated instead of satisfied.

Above all else, concentrate your time and limited resources toward achieving transactional efficiency on the Web site from the user's perspective. Solicit advice from accomplished individuals in the target market about the appearance and functionality of your proposed design and incorporate as much of it as possible into the final product, testing thoroughly and repeatedly to ensure that all features perform as instructed.

21 North Main's premise for transforming a fragmented used-book market into a coherent distribution system is hardly an innovative application of Internet technology. It merely capitalizes on

what the Internet does best—effectively and efficiently uniting a defined, active, and dispersed community of interest. Without attempting to alter distribution channels, buyer behaviors, or the proven capabilities of the Internet, 21 North Main has chosen instead to harness the pervasiveness and power of the Internet itself, cooperating rather than competing with used-book dealers as an intermediary to libraries.

Chapter 9

A View from the Other Side of the Reference Desk

Anne T. Keenan
Blair Public Library
annek@esu3.org

The Blair Public Library is located in Blair, Nebraska, a town with a mixed agricultural and industrial base and a population of 7,558. Blair is essentially an upper middle class community, with an unemployment rate of only 1.8 percent.

The Blair Public Library began offering public Internet access in the spring of 1997, and as of this writing we have two public access computers. Our Library's policy states that patrons can use the Internet for 30 minutes, but if no one is waiting to use it they can stay on as long as they please. In 1998 we recorded that 1,171 patrons accessed the Internet from our computers; by 1999, that figure had risen to 2,443. At this time, we do not use a filter on our Internet-enabled computers.

Patron Internet Use

By and large, patrons seem to learn quickly how to navigate to their favorite sites on the Web. The majority of patrons who access it are using free e-mail services such as Hotmail and joining chat groups. Older children often spend time playing games on the

Internet, and patrons with specific questions or with papers to write ask our Library staff for assistance. We've noted that the majority of users do not have very advanced searching skills, and though a number of research databases are advertised at the Library (such as Electric Library), they are rarely utilized. It's common for a patron to sit at a computer for a while and finally in frustration ask a librarian for assistance. Our staff spends an increasingly large part of each day either helping patrons find Web sites that they've heard about and/or finding information on databases for the patrons.

We've noticed that the Internet seems to draw two types of people. The first are those who spend a large part of their day there, enjoying their favorite sites. For the most part these patrons are not computer literate, therefore the librarians have to help them when they're trying to access new Web sites or unfamiliar material. The second group consists of those who come in occasionally and want information on a specific topic. Generally, they are familiar with the Internet but don't know how to access information. The majority of these patrons are shoppers. They want to buy car parts, exercise equipment, antiques on eBay, herbs, etc. Again, the librarians assist with these requests, helping the patrons find the requested Web pages.

Our Library has a staff of five and we've estimated that we each help an average of five Internet patrons a day. For the most part, our regular Internet patrons rarely use the other services available at the Library. They don't check out books, videos, or magazines; and they rarely participate in Library activities. At one time, it was suggested that providing Web access would motivate our customers to use the other services that we offer, but I've not found this to be true.

After e-mail and shopping, the Internet is used for locating quick facts. Patrons want to know where they can get a picture of the car that won a particular Nascar race in 1997, how to find when the ship *The Empress of Ireland* sank, and if they can get the words to a song. The average patron very quickly gets bored looking for information. A common complaint is that they are "wasting too much time searching" on the Web; again, the librarians assist in this search for material.

Web Site Utility

Once patrons locate a Web page, what makes them return and use the data offered?

I believe it starts with the Web page itself. The page should be light-colored and the text easy to read. What looks like navy blue text with a soft blue background on the Web page monitor may be impossible to read or copy on the user's printer. At least once a day a patron is unable to copy information because the colored text against the matching background is not visible on the Library printer.

When creating a Web page the author should avoid busy back-grounds. Graphics of dogs running across the screen and chang-ing colors are distracting and can actually detract from the infor-mation the site is trying to convey. The computer viewing the material might not have the memory or software that the Web designer's does. If the page is loaded with unnecessary or unusual graphics or sounds, the viewer will have to wait while their com-puter loads the information. It's quite possible that the user may become annoyed at the wait and leave the site entirely. It's also possible that the patron's computer will not have the memory to download the information at all, or the wait will cause the viewer's computer to time out of the site.

Another common complaint is that the Web site demands a spe-cific software program to access material. Often the suggested soft-ware is created by the designers of the Web page—if users down-loaded all the software these sites demanded, their computers would rapidly run out of memory. In addition, the chance of down-loading a virus is high. At the Blair Public Library we don't allow patrons to download except onto discs. Though we have anti-virus software in place, we can't take the chance that a patron might accidentally bring a virus to our Library computers. Some Web sites are not available at the Library for this reason.

Another common complaint is that our computers are not equipped with sound cards, because it was feared that the noise would be too distracting to the other patrons. As a result, some Web sites are not accessible to our users because their information is tied to sound cards and so cannot be downloaded to the host computer.

Web Evaluation

When training someone to use the Internet, we advise him or her to evaluate the site itself. How accurate is the information provided? Is there a way to verify the information in the database? There are no regulations for publishing on the Internet—that is both its strength and its weakness. The Web's advantage is that the average library can now offer many diverse views on any topic imaginable. Students are no longer isolated and limited to one opinion on a topic—they can study virtually the whole world.

However, the Web's downside is that anyone can publish on it. Along with the informative and scholarly Web sites, users have to sift through unlimited amounts of worthless material. Before the Internet, television producers, book publishers, newspaper editors, and librarians edited and distilled information for the average consumer. It is now up to the consumer to evaluate the worth of the information provided. Many people have difficulty with this; they believe what they read. Students commonly incorporate the information located on the Internet into their papers without paying any attention to the site itself. So the first question a patron needs to ask himself at a new site is whether the information provided is both accurate and error-free. When training patrons on Internet searching I always advise them to judge a Web site by evaluating the writing itself. If the quality of the writing is poor and if it seems to ramble and contain typo-graphical/grammatical errors, it's likely the author didn't bother to check his or her facts either.

A Web site that I enjoy is The Flat Earth Society (http://www.flat-earth.org). The Flat Earth Society's goal is to re-educate mankind, to disprove the common notion that the earth is round. I fre-quently use this site when demonstrating the do's and don'ts of searching on the Internet because it's a good example of poor data-base researching on the Internet. Even though I enjoy it, who pro-vides the information available in The Flat Earth Society database? What are his or her qualifications? Does he or she have any quali-fications other than an ax to grind?

I also caution patrons new to the Web to ask if the informa-tion offered is objective. Facts and statistics can be presented in such a way as to cause outrage. Does the site attempt to sway the reader in a certain direction or is it merely designed to inform or entertain? Does the site provide more than one point of view or links to other views on the same topic? How up-to-date is the information, and when was the last time it was updated? Is a bibliography of any type included with the mate-rial offered? Has the information offered been superceded or disproved by other individuals? Is this information available elsewhere on the Web and is the topic adequately covered? Who is the sponsor of the Web site, and why is the sponsor providing a Web site? Is there advertising at this site and what kind of advertising is it? Many Web sites are simply advertisements for products. The information included in the database is there only to convince the patron to buy the products listed. What kinds of links are there to related sites? Are the links from the site checked regularly and obsolete links deleted? Why would other people want to view this site?

Database Design

The information that the database covers should be clearly marked and indexed. A common failing I have noted of many genealogy Web sites is that they are not indexed in any way. Marriage, cemetery, and census records are increasingly being offered on these sites. However, when these records are accessed they are often simply a typed list of area records. The users can waste hours wading through the database searching for information that is not indexed in any way. Or more likely they will leave the database and not return.

Some indexed databases are not clear about the information they cover. A patron might fail to check the whole database because the information on the Web site does not clarify that the area where the patron is checking is only covering part of the database.

The database should also follow the same format throughout. Some databases are compiled by a number of different people who each used their own system. As the patron searches the database, the method of accessing the information is different from topic to topic.

The database should be easy to use. Many Internet users are new to computers and are intimidated by them. They are not accustomed to searching for information and are further handicapped by poor typing skills. They don't have the searching skills that a librarian has, and when researching a topic they might not know the exact name of the material they are looking for. Therefore the possibility for error is high, and spelling mistakes are common.

If at all possible the database should provide "close to" spellings so that users can scroll up or down the page to get to the citation or name that they want. The more points of entry a database has (keyword, subject, sounds like) the easier the database is to use and the more it will be utilized.

Amazon.com is a good example of a commercial, user-friendly Web site. It searches all of its databases from one location, yet it offers the option of searching a specific database to lower the number of possible hits. Amazon.com also offers alternate Web links. It's easy to limit or broaden a search, and customers can search by author, title, and subject. If searching for an antique or a CD or a book, the search method is clearly marked and essentially the same. It has advertising, but the ads are not intrusive and the response time of the database is fast. Another positive feature of the Amazon.com Web site is that patrons don't have to move from page to page to page to get the information they want. Some sites are like complicated mazes—users stumble around until finally in frustration they leave the site entirely. Graphics are also available at Amazon.com. The books and materials for sale can be viewed, but to save downloading time the customer controls the graphics. The users can click to see the cover of a book and even enlarge it, but not wait for their slower computer to download the color picture unless they so choose.

A common problem when searching Web sites is that often a page is up before the database is completed. I know individuals who think they're creating interest in their site by putting one up that's under construction. People don't like to go to a site that promises information only to discover that other than a very polished page no information or links are available. Users do not bookmark a site that's under construction; often they'll leave it and never go back.

Another complaint against many Web sites is that they offer e-mail addresses but never bother to respond to the users' questions. If an e-mail address is offered mail should be checked weekly (at the minimum) and the patrons' questions should be answered in a timely manner.

A person creating a Web database should also be aware that it's common practice to use them to cheat. Many students, rather than using the database for homework, are plagiarizing the information available. For example, I have been very excited about the bilingual sites. They open up new possibilities for understanding on a global scale. However, I also know of instances where students are using the sites that translate simple stories or fairy tales and claiming the translation as their own. If at all possible, when creating a database try to offer the information so that the average student will be forced to write his or her own paper, not just copy information from the Internet.

The World Wide Web is still a new service, and its potential is still being realized. It's changing the way people live and work. In the late 1950s commercial television was introduced and at that time no one knew what direction it would take. Would it be used for education, sports coverage, news, or pure entertainment? Since then it has proven that it can accommodate all of these things. The Web is comparable to television in its infancy. It is a very exciting time, and we're still deciding what we want the Web to be. Librarians are leading the way in this decision. Up to now newspapers, books, radio, and television have always been controlled by a select few because of the cost constraints formerly related to publishing. The Web was designed so that anyone can publish, and librarians are creating sites and training patrons. It's a wonderful opportunity and a great responsibility as we move into a new era.

Chapter 10

What Price Simplicity: A User-Centered Meditation

Laura B. Spencer

Paul Robeson Library

Rutgers University-Camden

laspence@crab.rutgers.edu

I want it all. I want it now. I don't want to wait for it, work for it, or spend any money for it. With everything being available on the Web, how hard could it be to obtain what I want on these terms and this timetable? After all, my assignment is due tomorrow.

Such misguided optimism exasperates librarians no end. It is an endlessly recurring, uphill battle to explain to impatient people with high expectations why the terms and timetable are unrealistic. There is just enough evidence of free, fast, and full-text on the Web to support their optimism.

The Trouble with Success

This problem, I would argue, is less a sign of something having gone wrong as much as having gone right in the electronic information environment. We are victims of our own successes. But success seems to exact a price. If you have read *Why Things Bite Back: Technology and the Revenge of Unintended Consequences* by Edward Tenner (New York: Knopf, 1996) you know that sometimes problems avenge themselves through their very solution. For example, we implement labor- and time-saving computer technology, only to spend hours trying to get the software to do a task that a secretary could once have done, quite without a computer's help, in but a few minutes. Then we hire technicians to fix the computer at three times the salary of the clerk for whom the computer was intended to replace. This doesn't seem to be progress at all.

Misplaced pessimism might throw up its hands in despair at this paradoxical and irritating outcome. But a return to the allegedly simpler days would likely create its own revenge effect. A more realistic approach to the problems that are the result of solutions is to be alert to their existence, expect their arrival, and prepare to address them more promptly than either optimism or pessimism is likely to do.

What kinds of problems should we be preparing to address after a database's successful migration to the World Wide Web? For the most part, the Web versions appear to be an improvement over their previous forms. CD-ROM databases tend not to be particularly transparent to operate, and print indexes are cumbersome and time-consuming. Web databases can have clean and spare interfaces, and be fairly easy to use with a minimum of instruction.

Even a novice can construct search strategies that will retrieve a large quantity of citations. He or she has plenty of choices, makes them, and can go away reasonably happy with the result. Database searching on the Web is a fairly straightforward process, which should be welcome news. What then, could the bad news be? What is biting us back? What is the hidden, avenging complexity of this Web-based simplicity, and what are its ramifications for us and for the people we serve?

I work in two academic libraries: Hahnemann Library at MCP/ Hahnemann University in Philadelphia, Pennsylvania, and Paul Robeson Library at Rutgers University in Camden, New Jersey. Most of the users I see are students, whose ages and database-searching skills range widely. Middle-aged returning students (whether at the graduate or undergraduate levels) tend to be new to conducting serious library research in an electronic environment, while some of the 18 to 22-year-old undergraduates appear to be new to conducting serious library research in any environment. How has the Web simplified, and how has it newly complicated, their work?

The Collapse of Space

In both institutions, the university libraries' home page is usually the student researcher's first port of call. With but a few clicks of the mouse, they can launch a search into any one of a large number of databases. This clean, simple interface is also flat, denying them the assistance of any spatial or tactile clues. The archives of knowledge and information have, in an electronic environment, collapsed into a very small physical space. In a sprawling paper-based environment, even the most confused student can learn that the history books are "over here" while the science books are "down there" and walk to the appropriate area when the need arises. Even the most impatient student can easily, if not necessarily happily, grasp the clear distinction between owned and not owned. In an electronic environment, much is almost but not quite there, and it is a frustrating puzzle for our students to understand what is available with just one click, with a sequence of clicks, a few clicks and a trip up the stairs or down the hall, or with a sequence of clicks plus a two-week wait. The collapse of physical space that is the genius of the electronic environment has inadvertently exacerbated the user's natural state of confusion.

There is a saying, "all time is now." From the perspective of a Web surfer, "all space is here." That is astoundingly convenient, but it allows for no geographical or spatial sense of the arrangement of knowledge. If that sounds like a weird or silly way to think about how information is stored or thought about, think about a messy desk—either yours, or, if you are one of the tidy people, your coworker's. (I'm sure you know at least one person who's on the messy side.) How do you find stuff on a messy desk? I find things on my messy desk because I have a sense of where the desired items are in space. A desired item is near a like item, either by subject or by priority level.

The nearness is physical, tactile, spatial. An electronic environment effectively removes those physical, tactile, and spatial mnemonics that work so well in finding items on messy desks. To put it in the terms of our profession, it removes an access point for retrieval. Students who are trying to find their way around the myriad of databases available to them have one less means to distinguish one from another. We would do well to consider this collapse of space to be not only a great gain, but a loss as well, and seek out compensatory measures for our users.

Yes, they could read the directions, the helpful headings and other clues that appear on the screen, or click on the little icon that will tell them what this or that database is used for. But adding clues or hints to the screen runs the risk of cluttering it. Besides, the student is often at a loss to know which tidbit to pay attention to, and which he or she may safely ignore. It is difficult to perceive a hierarchy of importance on a flat screen, because it is difficult to establish that hierarchy and display it when research priorities will differ from user to user.

The Compression of Time

Since the database is sorely limited in pointing out the right direction for searchers to go, databases bear greater responsibility for bringing focus and clarity to the act of searching, at precisely the time they are least prepared to do so. Searching a database on the Web, which tends to be so much easier and faster than searching its print or CD-ROM forebears, exacts its price by requiring the user to spend time and effort at a premature and unexpected moment. My experience is that, while users grumbled about using CD-ROM products, and sometimes sought to avoid the more unwieldy ones if possible, the difficulties came as no surprise. Web databases, I think, surprise them when their ease of use conceals difficulties in using them.

Students who surf the Web are accustomed to retrieving a lot of Web sites with very few keystrokes and not much more thought. From their point of view, why should the segment of the World Wide Web that the library home page connects to—i.e. the restricted databases—behave any differently?

Try to explain that difference to a student in a hurry to leave the premises or to finish this segment of his or her research task. Try to explain—especially to students studying to be healthcare professionals—that they cannot have it all now; they must think and sift first. Yes, they can learn with experience what kind of efforts they must exert, and what lengths of time are required, but they will circumvent the process whenever they can, as it is at odds with the sense of time demanded by their future professions, and at odds with the World Wide Web they believe they know. At the very time that unprecedented vast quantities of information are at or near their fingertips, their inclination and ability to exploit them will recede, owing to their surprise and impatience. More than once I have heard, "I thought this was supposed to save me time." It is a challenge to explain that it really and truly does, when their sense of time and effort to spend collide with the reality of searching databases on the Web.

The Web is supposed to save time. What time does it save? Among other stretches of time, it saves those tiring, prolonged moments of trying to get a CD-ROM database to produce a manageable body of relevant citations. How does the user generate those references in a CD-ROM environment? Assemble terms, fuss with an interface, try to remember which command sequences and which function keys fulfill his or her purpose. Finally, generate a list of citations, track down articles, and read them. The act of assembling and fussing might teach him or her something about the controlled vocabulary that database employs, which might help in future searches, even without the user being aware of learning anything of the sort.

A CD-ROM database search takes work and effort, which takes time. The user is thinking, however reluctantly or ineffectively, about his or her topic. The seeming opacity of the search interface forces the user to think at least a little. So the work of thought is interspersed with the work of mechanical, technical manipulations during the search process.

In a Web environment, by contrast, the mechanics are—or appear to be—nearly effortless. The thought process is less forced and more chosen. Ease of use requires little skill or thought. It becomes easy to forget that thought—thinking about the topic—is still appropriate, necessary, and desirable. The Web database no longer forces users to think about their topic, so they must deliberately choose to think about it at this point.

Making the choice to think strikes me as rather unlikely. I think it is the nature of most students—and most people, for that matter—to defer serious thought as long as possible. Muddle-headedness or foggy-mindedness is less a character flaw and more the natural state of a student at the early stages of a research process. Web databases' terrific and welcome successes in compressing time spent and reducing effort expended can produce a bottleneck effect in the student's head early on in the research process by requiring a clarity of mind that is extremely difficult to achieve. We would do well to be alert to this bottleneck, and take steps to lessen the pressure. Such steps might require that we penetrate more deeply into the student's thought process, which might not always be pleasant for either party. In the long run, though, I think it helps.

In the long run, Web databases save much time and effort, only to require that more time and effort be spent. The "long run" has not shortened as much as it first appears, either for users or for librarians, as both of us have new work to do. This revenge effect can be highly exasperating for all parties. What can lessen the exasperation is to think of the revenge as recompense. The new expenditures of time and effort are—to use terminology from the health professions—not failures of outcome to lament but chronic conditions to manage. Rather than waste our time and energy trying to either remove or deny the revenge effects, we can invest our time and effort into providing the necessary compensation to users so that they can get on with their work.

Chapter 11

Data and Metadata: An Overview of Organization in Searchable Full-Text Databases

Aurora Ioanid
Head of Bibliographic Control
Guggenheim Memorial Library
Monmouth University
aioanid@monmouth.edu

Vibiana Bowman
Reference Librarian
Robeson Library
Rutgers University-Camden
bowman@crab.rutgers.edu

Introduction

The mission of a cataloger is to sort and organize information. In order to describe, classify, analyze, and encode the knowledge condensed in books and periodicals, or other corresponding media, indexers and catalogers over the centuries have created a network of taxonomic terms. Examples of these control devices include controlled vocabulary, subject headings, classification schemes, indexing terms, etc. These schemes worked well until the late 20th century. Suddenly, there was an explosion of information due to a variety of factors, such as the invention of the computer, the advent of the Internet, and the proliferation of personal computers in the home. The Information Age has precipitated the need for new strategies in information storage, retrieval, and accessibility. In response to this need, people invented metadata, which simply put, means data about data.

"Metadata" are structured data that describe the characteristics of a resource. The term "meta" derives from the Greek word denoting a nature of higher order or more fundamental kind (Taylor, 1999). The Anglo-American Cataloguing Rules (AACR2) and the Dublin Core are two well-known metadata schemes. Fundamentally, metadata consist of two elements:

1. The information inherent to the material itself (title, author, physical description, etc.)

2. Information artificially appended to the metadata (subject, call number, uniform titles, etc.)

The success of the various schema can be measured, at least partly, by whether their inherent logic can be easily utilized to easily retrieve information.

A Short History of Metadata

The Card Catalog

One of the first organizational schemes utilized was the library catalog, which dates back to antiquity. Originally, catalogs were handwritten with spaces left to add new entries. At the end of the 19th century came the invention of the Dewey Decimal System. This organizational scheme standardized how books were shelved and cataloged. In addition, it provided a tool for the creation of the card catalog. The use of cards solved the problem of keeping the catalog up-to-date. Now each new listing could be easily added to the proper place in a file. In 1901 the Library of Congress began selling its catalog cards. Since then, many libraries have come to rely on the Library of Congress as their primary cataloging source and, over the years, the Library of Congress has come to serve as a centralized cataloging agency ("Library Cataloging," 2000).

With the advent of the computerized catalog new methods of searching became possible—for example, keyword searches and the ability to connect search terms with Boolean operators. The user now had access to the metadata, the various fields that catalogers used to describe the book (e.g., the date of publication, the language the book was written in, and even where in the library or library system the item was physically stored).

The computerized catalog freed the user from relying solely on the subject heading for access to a material by topic. Instead of consulting volumes of *Library of Congress Subject Headings,* the user could now search for a topic using the "first word that comes to mind" approach. In addition, the computer did more than provide the user with a quick and effective searching tool. It served to subtly change the art of cataloging. Where once catalogers were primarily concerned with producing entries for a catalog, they were now creating a database that could be easily searched by patrons ("Library Cataloging," 2000).

Indexes to Journals

Like books, periodicals presented a challenge to the researcher trying to access information through a subject approach. Subject heading, author, and title accesses have long been provided by paper indexes. That well-used standard, *The Readers Guide to Periodical Literature,* goes back to the 1890s. Bound indexes served their purpose well into the last part of the 20th century. But with the number of periodicals increasing dramatically, faster access and the compilation of results became a goal.

Law firms were among the first organizations to utilize electronic information retrieval. A literature search of articles related to database construction in the late 1980s and early 1990s reveals that the first "how-to" articles were written by law professionals. The reams of documents associated with legal practice served as the "necessity is the mother of invention" spur for law librarians to investigate better methods of accessing the information that they were called on to provide daily.

The next logical candidates for keyword searching and full-text access were the journal databases. For a researcher to have the ability to search for individuals' names, events, and topical issues and then to have the full text of a document displayed was, as Hamlet says, "a consummation devoutly to be wished." ProQuest Direct, a subsidiary of Bell & Howell Information and Learning began producing full-text/full-image CD-ROM products for periodical literature searching in 1988. In 1994, it offered a dial-up service, which provided keyword searching and full-text article display. ProQuest became Web-accessible in 1995. Similarly, Ovid Technologies was incorporated in 1988 as CD Plus, offering keyword searches and full article access. In 1992 CD Plus became available online, and in 1995 became Ovid Technologies. Thus, the online tools that professional researchers have come to rely on are relative newcomers in the field of information retrieval.

The world of electronic texts, and in particular that of the journal databases, presents special problems for commercial vendors. Descriptors and subject fields are still offered as part of the search process. Usually a search by descriptor is found under one of the "advanced search" features. Assigning subject headings is a costly and labor-intensive process. The controlled vocabulary of periodical databases is also known as an authority list. However, authority lists are not standardized from vendor to vendor, since they are produced for specific products.

Data, Metadata, and the Internet

The Internet has had far-reaching implications for the world of information storage and retrieval. Its profound lack of consistency, the way it embraces anarchy, and its easy access are the primary features that make it so appealing and so irritating at the same time. This is especially true for information professionals whose task it is to find some logical way to compose the most successful search strategies to get the most meaningful search results. How then to order the chaos?

While the world of the Internet may have the veneer of the old Wild West, its underpinnings are based in the eminently logical world of computer programming.

HTML (Hypertext Markup Language), which is the basis of Internet communication, is a subset of the SGML (Standard Generalized Markup Language), which became an international standard in the 1980s. HTML encodes electronic texts to an exquisite level of detail and thereby renders them researchable. Different search engines utilize different approaches to data organization. Yahoo! was one of the first directory approaches to the information on the Web.

In 1994 two graduate students (Jerry Yang and David Filo) constructed a navigational tool for the fledgling World Wide Web. That tool, Yahoo! (Yet Another Hierarchical Officious Oracle), which could be considered a rudimentary catalog of the Web, became one of the most financially successful start-ups on the Internet ("The History of Yahoo!," 1999).

Most researchers on the Web have had occasion to lament the high degree of irrelevant hits that often result from an Internet search. However, the Web, while not in its infancy, is certainly still in its childhood and its searching tools are becoming increasingly more sophisticated. Ask Jeeves is a search tool that was designed by linguists to utilize and recognize the patterns of natural language queries. Ask Jeeves' creators, Garrett Gruener and David Warthen, set out in the late 1980s to devise a "prototype question-answering service" ("What Is Ask Jeeves?," 2000) that was simple to use, where the user did not have to construct Boolean queries, and that produced relevant results. By

1997, Ask Jeeves was available in its initial format. By 1999, Ask Jeeves was getting positive reviews in the industry literature.

An abundance of search tools are available. Some, like Metacrawler, search across the Web and return results from a large number of different search engines. The Internet presents a new world of possibilities and calls for creative approaches to information organization and retrieval.

In considering the type of schema that can be used, you must consider the types of material that you are trying to organize. On the Internet, electronic databases will be dealing with the past discourse of human experience (historical works) as well as the contemporary discourse (ongoing, current research), all of which need to be accessed in some logical manner. The question then shifts from one of availability of material to the "findability" of the material. As every good researcher knows, even if something is owned, if it cannot be located it is of no use. Perhaps even more frustrating is when a plethora of data is retrieved, the researcher knows what she wants is there, but she has to wade through a sea of irrelevant data to get to what is needed. The analogy of trying to get a bunch of gerbils to queue up in parade formation comes to mind. Relevancy and accessibility are therefore of paramount importance in retrieving data. How this can be achieved in historic and contemporary documents will be considered next.

The Past Discourse Online

HWÆT WE GARDE
na in geardagum beodcyninga. (Kiernan, 1996)

As the above excerpt from *Beowulf,* the oldest extant English language epic poem, exemplifies, language is a fluid, evolving entity with constant shifts in spelling, meaning, and nuance. The farther removed in time the reader is from the source material the more difficult it is to construct search query for searching a full-text database. *Beowulf* is written in Old English, which is basically a foreign language when compared with Modern English. Which spelling should be used? How to handle words that have dramatically changed meaning? Should indexes be constructed to cross-reference old and modern usage? A myriad of problems, both technological and taxonomic, spring to mind begging answers.

The ability to search a document's full text in an electronic database is a highly touted event in the world of information technology. Users can search the metadata, the data, or a combination of the two. One initiative actively engaged in creating electronic resources for scholars is the Center for Electronic Texts in the Humanities (CETH). CETH was established by Rutgers and Princeton in 1991. Its mission is to "advance scholarship in the humanities through the use of high-quality electronic texts" ("Frequently Asked Questions...," 2000). One such product is the English Poetry Database.

The English Poetry Database, which contains over 165,000 poems from more than 1,250 poets from the years 600 to 1900, represents the complete English poetic canon from Anglo-Saxon times up to the end of the 19th century with the full text of each poem included. The anonymous author of *Beowulf* is included, as are all the notables such as Spenser, Donne, and, of course, Shakespeare. This canon is searchable by Keywords, Author, Poem Title, etc.—all the usual access methods for locating materials. If a researcher does a search by keyword, that word will be displayed in context. For example John Donne's poem "Love and Wit" begins "Trew love fynds wytt" in some versions and "True love finds wit" in others. Does the searcher use the archaic spelling "trew" or the modernized "true?" In the English Poetry Database a search on either term "and" Donne will result in a display that includes the desired poem, "Love and Wit." A considerable accomplishment.

The Web page for CETH (http://www.scc01.rutgers.edu/ceth) provides a wealth of information regarding the project, the strategies used, and general information about computing in the humanities. CETH scans an authoritative text and, using the standards of SGML and the TEI (Text Encoding Initiative), tracks and tags the elements of the text. While concordances have been available via computers for decades, CETH is moving full-text searching in the humanities to a higher level of searching flexibility and sophistication. Interestingly, the English Poetry Database does not provide the user with any controlled vocabulary, but organizes and limits the searches through the use of the tagged metadata (e.g., Poem, Title of Poem, Author Name, etc.).

Projects like The Complete Works of Shakespeare (http://www.chemicool.com/Shakespeare) from MIT provide search tools that permit the user to search all of Shakespeare's works for the occurrence of a particular word. For example, if a user types in the word "beard," the system will return a list that includes the search word quoted in context from the play as well as the plays listed in alphabetical order. The utility of such search functions for scholars is immeasurable.

The difference in the delivery and retrieval methods between manual searching and electronic searching is comparable to starting a fire with sticks and turning on a gas stove. The full text of the material (the data) is now organized and provides the user with almost instant gratification with the click of a mouse through the use of the metadata scheme. The major downside of this process is that the results became somewhat fuzzy, the problem of false hits. Less exact language produces less exact results.

The Contemporary Interdisciplinary Materials Online

In today's scholarly literature the boundaries among disciplines seem increasingly elastic. Common crossover fields are searches in Social Work, Psychology, and Education or Business, Psychology, and Social Sciences. Journals are moving toward an electronic environment and libraries are moving in the same direction. More and more commercial and non-commercial information providers, if not exclusively in the electronic environment, at least have a foot in both worlds: print and cyberspace.

In order to address the growing number of full-text, electronic, and cross-disciplinary scholarly literature, the need for some standardized format becomes apparent. A consistent, formulaic, sound strategy is crucial for indexing data in order to be able to retrieve it. A schema of controlled vocabulary seems a logical candidate.

Controlled Vocabulary as a Communication Tool

It all comes down to communication. People have always needed to communicate, orally and symbolically. Humans devised various codes: language, alphabets, music, art, etc. Every human language is based on a logical schema. Patterns and predictability are cornerstones of language. English is a difficult language to master because it is a pastiche of so many other languages. Spelling in English is even worse. But, for all its eccentricities, English does have patterns, a grammar, and syntax. Implicit in every language is a covenant between the speakers that words have agreed-upon meanings. The four-legged mammal that catches mice and sleeps all day is a "cat" in English, "chat" in French, and "katze" in German. This consistency of meaning enables communication.

As culture and technology become more complicated and diversified so does the language used to describe these phenomena. While these layers of complexities add to the richness of language, it also adds an element of confusion. A controlled vocabulary in the world of information science is an attempt to standardize the words used to find information. Thus, if a researcher is searching for "AIDS-Disease" he will not get results including articles about aids to increase the physical mobility of the patients in therapy, or audiovisual presentation aids.

In addition to its basic functions of information retrieval and storage, a controlled vocabulary also has a sociological/educational purpose. A quick check of *The Readers' Guide to Periodical Literature* from the turn of the century to the present is a mini-course in the evolution of American societal attitudes toward topics such as sex. For example, "prostitution" is cross-referenced with "freelove."

Morphology of Controlled Vocabulary

The morphology of controlled vocabulary, the study of its structure and form, is tied into these sociological/educational aspects, specifically to the descriptive and prescriptive aspects of a controlled vocabulary.

The descriptive function of a controlled vocabulary reflects the preferred term for a concept then in use. This is a dynamic process and incorporates both temporal and factual aspects. Facts sometimes change over time. Descriptions of new knowledge are dependent on the language in current use and changes slowly over time as the new knowledge is incorporated into the mainstream. For example, *The Readers' Guide to Periodical Literature* for 1890–1899 has a half-column listing for "Moving Pictures." Under that is a heading "Moving Pictures, Talking *See* Kinetophonograph." Not surprisingly, the February 2000 edition reflects the changes in the industry and its prominence in the social culture over the past century in the U.S. The subject heading, "Motion Pictures" with all its various subheadings encompasses eight pages of reviews, industry-related articles, and personality profiles in periodicals from popular entertainment magazines to scholarly journals.

The prescriptive function of a controlled vocabulary is concerned with the social aspects of language. The controlled vocabulary serves to codify acceptable use for a particular concept. For example: Homosexuality. Using *The International Index to Periodicals* as a source of indexing terms, the use of the term "Homosexual" and its various permutations were tracked. In the 1907–1915 edition none of the terms "gay," "homosexual," or "lesbian" appear. In the 1935–1937 volume neither "homosexual" nor "gay" is used. There is one reference to "Lesbian Greek, *see* Greek Language." The term "homosexuality" was being used in the 1955 edition but not "gay" or "lesbian." By 1975 *The International Index to Periodicals* had become *The Social Science Index*. There was one listing under "Gay Liberation Movement," several under "Homosexuality," but still no listings under "Lesbians." The 1995 edition has three pages of entries under the term "Gay." There are also two columns of entries using the heading "Lesbian" and two columns of entries that utilize the term "Homosexual." Interestingly, the subject heading "Social Identity" is now being used in a way that differs from the 1975 edition. In 1975 that term was used to describe articles about identification with a particular social group (based on ethnicity, class, economics, etc.). By 1995, the term was being used to identify gender identity issues.

It is interesting to speculate what the historical changes in the use of terms to describe homosexuality indicate about changing social attitudes. At the beginning of the century there is no search term to describe homosexuality in the index that covers scholarly research journals. It isn't easy for the modern scholar to find articles dating back to that period because of the lack of a common language and common understanding of the concept. The closest one can come to research on the topic is buried under headings such as "Sexual Hygiene" and "Sex Crimes." A shift in attitude seems to be noticeable in indexing terms after the Kinsey Report in the 1950s. Scholarly articles are being written and indexed under the terms preferred by the gay community. It could be posited that the controlled vocabulary reflects and perhaps helps to bring about change in this prescriptive function.

Structure and Relationships in Controlled Vocabulary

Often a subject heading will be cross-referenced, and the cross-reference aids the searcher in refining her search. There is again an educational element in the cross-referencing scheme. For example, if a student were researching the use of mustard gas in World War I trench warfare, he may start out using a keyword catalog search (e.g., "World War I" and "Gas"). This would lead him to the Library of Congress Subject Heading "World War, 1914–1918—Chemical Warfare." Should that prove too specific, he could move up the scheme to the broader heading "Chemical Warfare—History-20th Century."

Thus, a controlled vocabulary like the *Library of Congress Subject Headings* can have a two-fold purpose. It can provide a tool for the researcher to broaden or narrow her topic. It will also lead the researcher to related fields of knowledge with cross-referencing items whose initial connection may not be readily apparent.

Conclusion

The history of librarianship has been devoted to the organization of human knowledge. The search query is one of the main tools of librarianship to access that knowledge, and it usually uses either keywords or a controlled vocabulary. The keyword search will retrieve a large quantity of information, making use of the Boolean operators "and," "or," and "not" as instruments for widening or narrowing the search. It will be reasonably efficient in smaller databases, but as the quantity of information grows it will become more and more semantically unclear and irrelevant. In a controlled vocabulary structure, the keyword itself becomes part of that structure (the metadata) in the shape of a cross-reference.

The next major area for study and research is most likely the issue of the qualitative aspects of the search results. Some search engines and indexes already have mechanisms in place for ordering results on relevance. The creation of search tools that produce both highly specific and highly relevant results would do much to order the wealth of information available in this Information Age.

The dream is that the Internet will come to serve as the library to the world and the storage house for our collective human experience. Implications for catalogers, indexers, and reference professionals are staggering. Envision a multidimensional, multilanguage, and multimedia reference tool encompassing past discourses, the contemporary interdisciplinary ideas, and available full text. That dream is coming true.

References

"The Complete Works of Shakespeare," (1999).: http://www.chemicool.com/Shakespeare.

Davis, Michael C. (1998). "Knowledge Management." *Information Strategy: The Executive's Journal,* 15: 11-32.

"Frequently Asked Questions About Electronic Texts." (2000). *The CETH Homepage.* http://scc01.rutgers.edu/ceth.

"The History of Yahoo!" (1999).: http://join.yahoo.com/overview.html.

Johnson, Elmer D. and Michael H. Harris (1976*). History of Libraries in the Western World.* Metuchen, NJ: The Scarecrow Press.

Kiernan, Kevin, ed. (1996). "Resources for Studying Beowulf." *The Electronic Beowulf Project:* http://www.georgetown.edu/irvinemj/english016/beowulf/beowulf.html.

Lerner, Fred (1998). *The Story of Libraries: From the Invention of Writing to the Computer Age.* New York: Continuum.

"Library Cataloging," Encyclopedia Britannica (2000).: http://search. eb.com.

Muddamalle, Manikya Rao (1998). "Natural Language Versus Controlled Vocabulary in Information Retrieval." *Journal of the American Society for Information Science,* 49 (1998): 881-88.

Oin, Jian (2000). "Semantic Similarities Between a Keyword Database and a Controlled Vocabulary Database." *Journal of the American Society for Information Science,* 51: 166-81.

Taylor, Chris (April 1, 1999). "An Introduction to Metadata," http:// www. library.uq.edu.au/iad/ctmeta4.html.

"What Is Ask Jeeves?" (2000).: http://www.askjeeves.com/docs/about/ WhatIsAskJeeves.html.

Chapter 12

XML: A Way Ahead for the Library Database?

Richard Gartner
Pearson New Media Librarian
Bodleian Library, Oxford, U.K.
rg@bodley.ox.ac.uk

Introduction

If nothing else, the projects covered in this book speak of the diversity of information that libraries serve up to their users, and the diversity of ways in which they store it. One library may use industrial-strength systems such as Oracle that cost tens of thousands of dollars, while others may put together databases using such standard warhorses as Microsoft Access, or even use freeware packages that cost nothing other than time and effort.

The picture is rather akin to the variation in cataloging techniques and practices around some 30 years ago, before MARC and the Anglo-American Cataloguing Rules (AACR2) appeared to rationalize approaches to describing the contents of libraries. Standardization of any type has its problems, and many catalogers found the introduction of MARC and its superseding of tried and tested methods traumatic—but the advantages of its approach are more than apparent these several decades later. The great union catalogs on which librarians rely so much, the sharing and exchange of records that reduce the burden of original cataloging for many institutions, and the collaborative projects that allow scholars such fast access to the great collections of the world would all be impossible if the initial steps toward standardization had not been taken in the 1960s.

Libraries are now beginning to reach the stage where the same imperatives that drove standardization in the area of cataloging are becoming apparent in the much more complex world of the digital content that they provide. Libraries now see it as part of their mission to compile databases for their users, often to accompany digital versions of their holdings, but also as useful services in their own right. Without any standardization of methods, especially in the area of the information formats, these databases are difficult to relate to one another. The cross-searching facilities that makes online catalogs so useful are hard to implement, and it is an onerous business for projects to exchange records with others to allow collaboration and the creation of union collections.

Oxford University's experiences in the early stages of its digitization work provide a pertinent illustration of some of the problems that this inconsistency of approach brings in its wake. At the time of writing, Oxford's libraries have completed a number of projects—these include their first completed digital collection of some 1,000 items of printed ephemera (known as the Toyota Project at http://www.bodley.ox. ac.uk/toyota); a substantial collection of digital images from its collection of Broadside Ballads (http://www.bodley.ox.ac.uk/ballads); and their largest project so far, the Internet Library of Early Journals (ILEJ; http://www.bodley.ox.ac.uk/ilej), a library of 18th- and 19th-century journals that include some 110,000 images. To these can be added a collection of very high-quality images of medieval manuscripts (http://image.ox.ac.uk), a database of the Bodleian Library's holdings of Modern Political Papers, finding aids detailing collections of the papers of former prime ministers, and a detailed analytical bibliography of the Bodleian Library's incunabula, among many others.

Looking at the methodologies employed by these projects reveals a bewildering array of approaches and techniques. The Toyota and ILEJ projects both use the Standard Generalized Markup Language (SGML), a scheme devised initially as a standard for marking-up electronic texts but now used as a means of holding information of all types. The Ballads projects uses a software package known as Allegro, which was initially designed to provide Chinese-language cataloging. The medieval manuscripts project encodes all its information directly in HTML (Hypertext Markup Language), the language used to mark up documents for the World Wide Web. The Modern Political Papers database and the lists of prime ministerial papers were initially input into the database package FoxPro, and are now in Microsoft Access—none are currently accessible over the Internet. The incunabula "database" is simply a collection of Microsoft Word files with tagging devised by the catalogers.

This is a relatively small number of projects, but already this diversity is beginning to present problems for the librarians and their users. It is not possible to perform simple cross searches across these digital collections—as can readily be done across the catalogs of Oxford's 100 or so libraries—by a single unified interface. Each database has to be accessed directly, navigated using its own interface, and the results of searches taken in whatever format it delivers. Many of these databases are on the Web and are readily accessible in physical terms, but a few reside on single machines within the library, requiring the users to visit them in person, in a manner akin to the card catalog of a pre-MARC library.

For the librarian, this diversity of approach also presents problems. The danger of entrusting a database compiled with great time and effort to a proprietary package is that such packages become obsolete with frightening rapidity, and the information they hold can become difficult if not impossible to retrieve and convert to the current state-of-the-art. Oxford had to spend some time converting databases compiled only a couple of years earlier to Microsoft Access when this became widespread and support for FoxPro, which had been the mainstay of database work within the library sector, fell out of favor. Packages in common use at the beginning of the 1990s are beginning to look like cuneiform tablets, increasingly inscrutable and mysterious. Databases need a robust format of guaranteed longevity if they are not to disappear into the ether as future technologies arise.

The librarian's problems continue when looking at the data itself. Different fields with different fieldnames, different approaches to recording names, subjects, and titles—these all make it difficult to contemplate providing a coherent way of accessing a growing mass of information. And if the librarian comes across another project covering much the same area, collaboration is going to be a problem. Even more than any technical problems arising from the use of incompatible software packages, records input to different standards are going to make the exchange or merging of records onerous and time-consuming.

Is there any chance of the in-house database achieving something of the consistency that MARC and AACR2 brought to the library catalog? It is a much more formidable challenge than the one that greeted catalogers in the 1960s. The information listed on the catalog record did not vary enormously from one institution to another, but even this relatively small degree of variation was enough to give the initial setters of the standard plenty of headaches. The range of information that any library database or digitization project may wish to encode is self-evidently much larger. Could this be a little ambitious, perhaps?

Certainly this is too ambitious for any single set of fields that anyone could attempt to compile. No one is going to encompass the full range of human knowledge in a single database, nor is anyone likely to succeed at even the much more modest task of describing every potential object contained within a library's collections. What we can at least do is devise a *framework* within which these elements can be placed, a logical and extensible backbone with a common center that will allow, at least at the basic level, some degree of inter-communication between the diverse objects contained within it.

Any framework that is going to perform this function will have to fulfill certain prerequisites. It will have to be nonproprietary, so that it will not bind our information to a given piece of software. It will have to be robust enough to be readable at some distant time in the future. It will have to be well structured, so as to allow the logical arrangement of our information in a way predictable enough to allow cross-searching, but also flexible, and above all extensible, to allow it to cope with new information that will mate-rialize in the future.

The term extensible points the way to a possible solution to this dilemma. The eXtensible Markup Language (XML) has the poten-tial to meet these requirements, and it is to an examination of the ways in which it could be used as a standard for a diverse mass of information that the rest of this chapter is devoted.

What is XML?

XML is a slightly simplified form of SGML, which has been around for over 30 years and it was devised by the International Standards Organization (ISO) as a standard for the marking up of electronic texts. The explanation below applies equally well to SGML and XML.

XML is a set of rules for defining a series of tags (known as ele-ments) that are used to encode texts when they are converted to electronic form. A sample of XML may look like this:

```
<poem>
    <title>carmen lxx</title>
    <author>Catullus</author>
```

```
<text>
      <line>nulli se dicit mulier mea nubere malle</line>
      <line>quam mihi, non si se Iuppiter ipse petat.</line>—
      <line>dicit: sed mulier cupido quod dicit amanti,</line>
      <line>in vento et rapida scribere oportet aqua.</line>
</text>
</poem>
```

The format of these tags may look familiar to anyone who has constructed a Web site, as they follow exactly the same convention as those used in HTML. The difference here is that instead of the tags merely indicating how the text they contain is to be displayed, as most of the HTML tags do, these indicate the *semantic* content of the text they enclose. In the example above, for instance, they show that the words "carmen lxx" are the title of the poem, and that "Catullus" is the name of the author. XML is clearly much more powerful than HTML in terms of what it can tell us about the text it encodes.

If you look at the formal definition for XML, however, what you will not find is a set of tags—it will not tell you to use <poem>, <title>, <author>, <text>, and <line> to mark up a poem as in the above example. XML is a set of rules telling us how to *define* these tags, what they look like and how they are structured, but it does not dictate their content. Before XML can be used, we have to define the tags we will be using, and a series of rules explaining what tag can go where within a document—these are what is commonly known as a *Document Type Definition* or DTD.

The diversity of possible information that can be marked up in XML dictates that different applications may require different DTDs to sensibly mark up the text they contain. The set of tags necessary to mark up poetry may well differ from that used for standard prose, and the set used to mark bibliographic information about a text (the metadata) may well be different again. It is no surprise, therefore, to find that a number of DTDs have been put together, all aimed at fulfilling different functions.

The most commonly used DTD in the world today is HTML, which is designed to instruct Web browsers how to display the documents marked up using its tag set. It comes as a surprise to many users of HTML that it is not a separate language, but merely an application of XML. Popular as HTML is, it is relatively poor in conveying much information about the text it encodes beyond instructions on its rendering. Two much more powerful DTDs are widely used for more demanding applications: the Encoded Archival Description (EAD; http://lcweb.loc.gov/eadhome) and the Text Encoding Initiative (TEI; http:// www.tei-c.org).

The EAD was designed by the Library of Congress and Society of American Archivists as a standard for the automation of archival finding aids. It incorporates an extensive set of tags for describing an archival collection as a whole, and also its component parts, down to the level of individual items. It is flexible enough to allow great variety in complexity and detail, and is already in heavy use for describing both traditional archives and digital collections.

The TEI is a longer-established scheme for marking up electronic texts of all types, and is the most widely used DTD for producing electronic editions of texts. It is a modular system, incorporating a base set of tags applicable to all types of text, and a number of optional tag sets for particular classes of material (such as poetry, technical manuals, dictionaries, or transcriptions of speech). In addition to tags for marking up the text itself, it also includes a large number for bibliographic information, much of which is designed to map to fields in the MARC format.

Unlike SGML, which usually requires conversion to another format before it can be viewed, XML is designed to be readily viewable by relatively simple browsers, using its partner language XSL (eXtensible Stylesheet Language) to format its tags for display. The next generation of Web browsers will be able to view

XML documents directly via this mechanism. Already Microsoft's Internet Explorer 5 can do this, although its use of XML is still rather basic. Future versions of other Web browsers will be able to do the same.

Using XML as a Database

Although it was initially devised as a way to mark up electronic texts, it is clear that XML can also function in ways analogous to a database. XML tags can function like database fields, and can be searched just like the content of a database field. Searches as complex as anything possible in a relational database (including Boolean searches) can be easily carried out on an XML file. A range of software packages, ranging from freeware (such as the excellent *sgrep* program, found at: http://www.cs.helsinki.fi/~jjaakkil/sgrep.html) to very powerful and very expensive search engines are already available for XML, and more are on the way, but at its very simplest an XML file can be searched using standard commands (such as grep in Unix) that come as part of an operating system.

XML does have major advantages over a relational database when it comes to its role as a standard. It is validated by the ISO as the prime method of encoding electronic texts, and several major DTDs (such as the EAD and TEI mentioned above) have become de facto standards in their fields. XML is also independent of any given software application and is entirely nonproprietary, reasons for which the Committee on Preservation and Access (Coleman, 1997) consider it the most robust format for the storage of data and metadata.

Because XML is written in standard ASCII code and not in a proprietary binary format, it can be read by many software packages and is readily interchangeable between applications. This means that it becomes a lot easier for a library to share its work in compiling a database with other institutions, either by directly loading each other's data, or by mapping elements from one XML file to another to allow cross-searching. XML allows the possibility for the first time of the type of cooperation in compiling databases that has been the norm for many years in automated cataloging.

XML also has the major advantage of simplicity when it comes to rendering some types of data. Because it is a hierarchical system, it allows data that has to be expressed in multiple levels to be integrated into the same file in a way that is much less complicated than linking a number of tables in a relational database. For example, a library may wish to describe a collection of papers, starting with a description of the entire collection, and working down from this level to sub-levels describing series within it, down to individual items and then components of items. Expressing this in a relational database is very complicated: using XML, all of this information can be integrated into a single file, making maintenance and portability much easier.

Using SGML/XML for a Major Image Database: The Internet Library of Early Journals

XML and its immediate antecedent SGML have been used successfully in several major digital library projects over the last decade. Some notable large-scale projects to use it include the Library of Congress' American Memory Project (http://memory.loc.gov), which uses a specially adapted version of the TEI and also the EAD for its finding aids; the Online Archive of California (http://sunsite2.berkeley.edu/oac), which uses the EAD; and Harvard University's Visual Information Access (http://via.harvard.edu:748/html/VIA.html) project, which uses a specially designed DTD to maintain a union catalog of visual resources at Harvard.

At Oxford University, SGML was used in the University Libraries' first completed digital imaging project, the Toyota Project, and more recently in the much larger-scale ILEJ Project. Although both used SGML, as XML had not been devised when they were put together, exactly the same principles would apply now if they were to use XML, and so they show well the potential of using this approach. We will look at the ILEJ project in more detail.

ILEJ was a joint project by the Universities of Birmingham, Leeds, Manchester, and Oxford, conducted under the auspices of the U.K.'s eLib (Electronic Libraries) Programme, which sought to kick-start digital library operations within the Higher Education Community by funding a few large-scale projects. It digitized substantial runs (10-20 years' worth) of six 18th- and 19th-century journals, including such key primary resources at the *Gentleman's Magazine* and *Notes and Queries*, and mounted these images on the Internet. In total, approximately 110,000 images were scanned, from original bound volumes in the case of four titles, and from microfilm surrogates in the case of two others. One of the rationales behind the project was to test out the problems presented by a wide variety of materials with differing technical challenges when it came to scanning, and differing requirements when it came to presentation.

In addition to the images themselves, the ILEJ project also involved the collection of a variety of metadata to accompany the scans. These included the standard bibliographic information for each volume and for each image that was necessary to allow the user to navigate the collection. In addition, for two titles the full text was provided in searchable form by means of uncorrected output from optical character recognition (OCR) software, and in the case of a few titles, the original printed subject indexes published contemporaneously with the journals themselves were converted into a searchable form by a keyboarding company. In total, 384 MB of metadata of a bewildering variety were compiled to accompany the images.

Although we experimented briefly with using a relational database package to hold this information, it quickly became apparent that it would be prove difficult to manage material of this size and complexity within a relational structure. Moving the metadata to SGML made things much simpler, and we found it easy to add new metadata to enhance the service by slotting them into the SGML structures we had decided upon.

The ILEJ project uses two DTDs, the EAD and the TEI—the EAD is used to describe the structure of the collection as a whole, and describe its contents down to the level of each physical volume (including the volume number and date of each item). To describe each item and its contents, the TEI is used—each file contains full information on each volume, including bibliographic data, pointers to each image file, converted subject indexes, and the full text of the volume where this is available. This variety of information slots neatly into a single file, which is much easier to search and process than the array of relational database tables that would otherwise be necessary to hold it.

The interface to the ILEJ journals was designed in-house and uses a powerful search engine, Opentext 5, to process the metadata and a number of scripts written in the Perl programming language to convert the SGML text to HTML for output to the Web. This reformatting requires a good deal of programming, but this should be largely obviated by XML, which will allow the results output by a search engine to be displayed directly in a Web browser. Experiments have already been carried out on an XML version of the ILEJ metadata, and they have shown that information is delivered to the user much more quickly, and with much less load on the library's server, when it is no longer necessary to carry out these cumbersome conversions. (More information on the ILEJ project's use of metadata can be found in the project's final report at http://www.bodley.ox.ac.uk/ilej/papers/fr1999.)

The Future: An Integrated Strategy for Metadata?

The problems for the librarian in the current free-for-all in terms of the way in-house databases are compiled have already been enumerated. These problems apply equally to projects such as ILEJ, where the metadata is used to retrieve images, as to more conventional databases, where it is the end point of the user's query. Does XML offer the possibility of standardizing the use of metadata within libraries, and so providing some of the advantages that the advent of standards in online cataloging have made possible?

XML offers major advantages over proprietary database technologies in its interchangeability, its lack of dependence on a given software system, its facilities for cross-searching, and its hierarchical approach to structure and its robustness. But to implement it on a library-wide basis requires some difficult decisions and a steep learning curve for librarians unused to this new way of thinking about data. Key decisions have to be made not only about which DTDs to use, but also *how* they are to be used, as few are so rigid that they can be implemented in one way only. To borrow an analogy from cataloging, not only do we have to devise an equivalent of the MARC standard but also an equivalent of AACR2 that will provide guidelines for the application of the standard. Only when both have been implemented does the possibility of true interchangeability become attainable. The task of defining standards to handle the variety of information that libraries can handle is, however, much more complicated than the relatively constrained world of the catalog record.

The choice of DTDs is a primary one, and it is a choice that can be bewildering when one surveys the large numbers that have already been devised. In addition to choosing a ready-made DTD, there is always the possibility of devising one's own, although this has disadvantages in terms of the complexity of the task and the loss of exchangeability with other applications that follows from using a unique DTD. An approach that seems to work well and uses well-established DTDs that already enjoy wide usage is the combined approach already taken by ILEJ. This uses the EAD for the description of the virtual collection down to a simple item-level description, and then an auxiliary DTD (in this case the TEI) where items have an internal structure or for other reasons require a more detailed level of description than the EAD provides. Both DTDs have proved flexible enough to handle the wide variety of metadata required of them, but are also well structured and defined enough to allow the vital inter-changeability that this area needs.

Drawing up a set of guidelines for implementing these DTDs is rather difficult. Their flexibility necessitates agreement on a set of standards on how they should be applied. Among the factors that have to be decided are which of their many optional elements should be used, what level of depth should be followed for cataloging, and what name authorities or classification systems should be followed. Fortunately, the task has been made easier by precedents already set by key figures in the world of metadata. Application guidelines for the EAD have been published by the Society of American Archivists (1999) and the Research Libraries Group (http://www.rlg.org/rlgead/guidelines.html), both of which provide useful guidance on the issues that have to be addressed when deciding on implementing the EAD itself. A similar set of guidelines for the TEI has been drawn up by a working group set up by the Digital Library Federation (http://www.indiana.edu/letrs/tei). These and other documents should form a useful basis for drawing up a set of local (but preferably more widely implemented) guidelines to allow the beginnings of a process of standardization in the treatment of metadata.

Moves toward this level of standardization are already under-way at Oxford, where the diversity of approaches toward digital library projects is causing problems even with the relatively small number of projects already completed. A working group has been set up specifically to devise a metadata scheme using XML that will apply to all digital library projects within Oxford University's libraries, and to draw up a set of "cataloging rules" to which all projects will have to conform. Once the scheme is fully drawn up, existing digital library projects within Oxford will be retroconverted to the new format, to ensure their integration with future projects. The end result of this process will be a single interface to all Oxford's digital projects to allow cross-searching and browsing at a basic level, in addition to project-specific interfaces that will allow additional features dictated by the requirements of the projects' respective materials. The scheme will also allow cross-searching from the University's central catalog, and also from sites outside Oxford that are able to access the XML-encoded material.

For true interoperability outside a single institution, a universally agreed-upon set of rules and standards are going to be required, as well as a support infrastructure for these standards analogous to that already existing for MARC and AACR2. The task is more ambitious than that which faced the designers of the cataloging standards, but the extensibility of XML, including its facilities for linking files together, means that a well-structured but modular system can be devised that should be able to cope with most requirements. Technically, everything is now in place for such a standard to be drawn up and implemented. XML is well defined, software is now available that provides search facilities of a speed and complexity that match those attained by the best traditional database systems, and suitable systems of name authorities and subject classifications are already in place.

The time is ready for the work already done on application guidelines for the DTDs mentioned above to be consolidated into an established standard, so allowing library database projects of all types to reach the next stage of maturity. This is a process that should not be over-delayed, as all those who went through retro-conversion projects of pre-MARC catalogs will testify that a large bulk of legacy data can be a daunting prospect. But at least by having our information in XML, encoded according to established DTDs, the process of later conversion to a universal standard will be that much easier.

References

Coleman, James (1997). *SGML as a Framework for Digital Preservation and Access.* Commission on Preservation and Access.

Society of American Archivists (1999). Encoded Archival Description Working Group. *Encoded Archival Description Application Guidelines Version 1.0.* Society of American Archivists.

About the Editor

Julie M. Still, currently a faculty member at the Paul Robeson Library, Rutgers University-Camden, has edited two previous books, written numerous articles, and given conference papers on a variety of topics in library science and history. She received an M.L.S. from the University of Missouri, Columbia, and an M.A. in history from the University of Richmond. Her research interests have focused primarily on reference and instruction, electronic resources and the Internet, and the humanities and social sciences.

The books Julie has edited, *The Internet Library*, *The Library Web*, and this title, have all been case studies of library and other nonprofit institutions' use of the Internet. She has authored and co-authored several articles, including an analysis of library Web site content and design (co-authored with Laura Cohen) that was published in *College & Research Libraries*. A study of the presentation of libraries and librarians in discipline-specific pedagogical journals, published in the *Journal of Academic Librarianship*, was awarded the New Jersey Library Association College and University Section's Research Award in 1999, and appeared on the American Library Association Library Instruction Round Table's Top 20 Articles on Library Instruction in the same year.

In 1997 Julie was featured in an article in the *Chronicle of Higher Education*. She has also published a number of articles in *Econtent* (formerly *Database*). A frequent conference speaker, she has presented papers at National Online Meeting, International Online Meeting, Computers in Libraries, and at state and local meetings. She lives with her family in Pennsylvania and is active in a variety of community groups.

Index

S

More Great Books
from Information Today, Inc.

Design Wise

A Guide for Evaluating the Interface
Design of Information Resources

By Alison Head

"*Design Wise* takes us beyond what's cool and what's hot and shows us what works and what doesn't."
>   —*Elizabeth Osder,*
>   *The New York Times on the Web.*

Knowing how to size up user-centered interface design is becoming as important for people who choose and use information resources as for those who design them. This book introduces readers to the basics of interface design and explains why a design evaluation should be tied to the use and purchase of information resources.

1999/224 pp/softbound • ISBN 0-910965-31-5 • $29.95
1999/224 pp/hardbound • ISBN 0-910965-39-0 • $39.95

The Evolving Virtual Library II
Practical and Philosophical Perspectives

Edited by Laverna M. Saunders

This new edition of *The Evolving Virtual Library* documents how libraries of all types are changing with the integration of the Internet and the Web, electronic resources, and computer networks. It provides a summary of trends over the last 5 years, new developments in networking, case studies of creating digital content delivery systems for remote users, applications in K-12 and public libraries, and a vision of things to come. The contributing experts are highly regarded in their specialties. The information is timely and presents a snapshot of what libraries are dealing with in the new millennium.

1999/194 pp/hardbound • ISBN 1-57387-070-6 • $39.50

The Library Web
Case Studies in Web Site Creation and Implementation

Edited by Julie M. Still

This is a superior collection of case studies of library Web projects, with an emphasis on Web page creation and maintenance. The contributors are from a variety of academic, special, and public libraries, and discuss a broad range of experiences. Coverage includes instructional materials, unique resources, and commercial Web design options. Programs and software for building a Web site are covered, as are issues in planning for a Web page and discussions of ways to involve all areas of the library in its evolution.

1997/230 pp/hardbound • ISBN 1-57387-034-X • $39.50

The Modem Reference, 4th Edition
The Complete Guide to PC Communications

By Michael A. Banks

"If you can't find the answer to a telecommunications problem here, there
 probably isn't an answer."

— Lawrence Blasko, The Associated Press

Now in its 4th edition, this popular handbook explains the concepts behind
computer data, data encoding, and transmission; providing practical advice for
PC users who want to get the most from their online operations. In his
uniquely readable style, author and techno-guru Mike Banks *(The Internet
Unplugged)* takes readers on a tour of PC data communications technology, explaining how modems, fax
machines, computer networks, and the Internet work. He provides an in-depth look at how data is communicated between computers all around the world, demystifying the terminology, hardware, and software.
The Modem Reference is a must-read for students, professional online users, and all computer users who
want to maximize their PC fax and data communications capability.

2000 • Softbound • ISBN 0-910965-36-6 • $29.95

Teaching with Technology
Rethinking Tradition
Edited by Les Lloyd

This latest informative volume from Les Lloyd includes contributions from
leading experts on the use of technology in higher education. Four sections are
included: Cross-Discipline Use of Technology, The Web as a Tool in Specific
Disciplines, Technology Management for Faculty and Administration, and
Techniques for Enhancing Teaching in Cross-Discipline Courses. If your college or university needs to be on the cutting edge of the technology revolution,
this book is highly recommended.

1999/400 pp/hardbound • ISBN 1-57387-068-4 • $39.50

Library Relocations and Collection Shifts
By Dennis Tucker

In *Library Relocations and Collection Shifts*, author, librarian, and move director Dennis
Tucker explains how to develop an appropriate moving plan for a library of any type or
size. A thorough revision of his classic, *From Here to There: Moving a Library*, the book
provides coverage of all these topics and more:

- Appointing a move director and committee
- Customizing a library moving plan
- Handling books and periodicals
- Working with professional movers
- Moving methods and strategies
- Planning and coordinating the move
- Cleaning, fumigation, and deacidification
- Communicating with staff and the public

You'll also find information on using spreadsheets to shift periodical collections, a sample
moving contract, a directory of useful resources, and suggestions for further reading.

1999/212 pp/hardbound • ISBN 1-57387-069-2 • $35.00

Beyond Book Indexing

How to Get Started in Web Indexing, Embedded Indexing, and Other Computer-Based Media

Edited by Marilyn Rowland and Diane Brenner

Are you curious about new indexing technologies? Would you like to develop and create innovative indexes that provide access to online resources, multimedia, or online help? Do you want to learn new skills and expand your marketing possibilities? In *Beyond Book Indexing*, edited by Diane Brenner and Marilyn Rowland, 12 articles written by 10 noted indexing professionals provide an in-depth look at current and emerging computer-based technologies and offer suggestions for obtaining work in these fields. Extensive references and a glossary round out this informative and exciting new book.

2000/150 pp/softbound • ISBN 1-57387-081-1
ASI Members—$25 Non-Members—$31.25

Great Scouts!

CyberGuides for Subject Searching on the Web

By Nora Paul and Margot Williams
Edited by Paula Hane
Foreword by Barbara Quint

Great Scouts! is a cure for information overload. Authors Nora Paul (The Poynter Institute) and Margot Williams (*The Washington Post*) direct readers to the very best subject-specific, Web-based information resources. Thirty chapters cover specialized "CyberGuides" selected as the premier Internet sources of information on business, education, arts and entertainment, science and technology, health and medicine, politics and government, law, sports, and much more. With its expert advice and evaluations of information and link content, value, currency, stability, and usability, *Great Scouts!* takes you "beyond search engines"—and directly to the top sources of information for your topic. As a reader bonus, the authors are maintaining a Web page featuring links to all the sites covered in the book.

1999/320 pp/softbound • ISBN 0-910965-27-7 • $24.95

The Extreme Searcher's Guide to Web Search Engines

A Handbook for the Serious Searcher

By Randolph Hock
Foreword by Paula Berinstein

Whether you're a new Web user or an experienced online searcher, here's a practical guide that shows you how to make the most of the leading Internet search tools. Written by leading Internet trainer Randolph (Ran) Hock, this book gives an in-depth view of the major search engines, explaining their respective strengths, weaknesses, and features, and providing detailed instructions on how to use each to its maximum potential. As a reader bonus the author is maintaining a regularly updated directory online.

1999/212 pp/hardbound • ISBN 0-910965-38-2 • $34.95
1999/212 pp/softbound • ISBN 0-910965-26-9 • $24.95

Super Searchers in the News

The Online Secrets of Journalists & News Researchers

By Paula J. Hane
Edited by Reva Basch

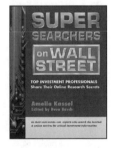

Professional news researchers are a breed apart. The behind-the-scenes heroes of network newsrooms and daily newspapers, they work under intense deadline pressure to meet the insatiable, ever-changing research needs of reporters, editors, and journalists. Here, for the first time, 10 news researchers reveal their strategies for using the Internet and online services to get the scoop, check the facts, and nail the story. If you want to become a more effective online searcher and do fast, accurate research on a wide range of moving-target topics, don't miss *Super Searchers in the News*. As a bonus, a dedicated Web page links you to the most important Net-based information sources—Super Searcher tested and approved!

2000/256 pp/softbound • ISBN 0-910965-45-5 • $24.95

Super Searchers on Wall Street

Top Investment Professionals
Share Their Online Research Secrets

By Amelia Kassel
Edited by Reva Basch

Through her probing interviews, Amelia Kassel reveals the online secrets of 10 leading financial industry research experts. You'll learn how information professionals find and analyze market and industry data, as well as how online information is used by brokerages, stock exchanges, investment banks, and individual investors to make critical investment decisions. The Wall Street Super Searchers direct you to important sites and sources, illuminate the trends that are revolutionizing financial research, and help you use online research as part of a powerful investment strategy. As a reader bonus, a directory of top sites and sources is hyperlinked and periodically updated on the Web.

2000/256 pp/softbound • ISBN 0-910965-42-0 • $24.95

Super Searchers on Health & Medicine

The Online Secrets of Top Health & Medical Researchers

By Susan M. Detwiler
Edited by Reva Basch

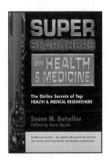

With human lives depending on them, skilled medical researchers rank among the best online searchers in the world. In *Super Searchers on Health & Medicine*, medical librarians, clinical researchers, health information specialists, and physicians explain how they combine traditional sources with the best of the Net to deliver just what the doctor ordered. If you use the Internet and online databases to answer important health and medical questions, these Super Searchers will help guide you around the perils and pitfalls to the best sites, sources, and techniques. As a reader bonus, "The Super Searchers Web Page" provides links to the most important Internet resources for health and medical researchers.

2000/208 pp/softbound • ISBN 0-910965-44-7 • $24.95

net.people

The Personalities and Passions Behind the Web Sites

By Eric C. Steinert
and Thomas E. Bleier

With the explosive growth of the Internet, people from all walks of life are bringing their dreams and schemes to life as Web sites. In *net.people*, authors Bleier and Steinert take you up close and personal with the creators of 36 of the world's most intriguing online ventures. For the first time, these entrepreneurs and visionaries share their personal stories and hard-won secrets of Webmastering. You'll learn how each of them launched a home page, increased site traffic, geared up for e-commerce, found financing, dealt with failure and success, built new relationships—and discovered that a Web site had changed their life forever.

2000/317 pp/softbound • ISBN 0-910965-37-4 • $19.95

Internet Blue Pages

The Guide to Federal Government Web Sites, 2001—2002 Edition

By Laurie Andriot

*"A handy, useful guide to federal government information
…comprehensive…authoritative…recommended."*

—CHOICE

Internet Blue Pages (IBP) is the leading guide to federal government information on the Web. *IBP 2001-2002* includes over 1,800 annotated agency listings, arranged in U.S. Government Manual style to help you find the information you need. Entries include agency name and URL, function or purpose of selected agencies, and links from agency home pages. With double the coverage of the previous edition, *IBP* now includes federal courts, military libraries, Department of Energy libraries, Federal Reserve banks, presidential libraries, national parks, and Social Security offices. A companion Web site features regularly updated agency links.

2000/464 pp/softbound • ISBN 0-910965-43-9 • $34.95

Electronic Styles

A Handbook for Citing Electronic Information

By Xia Li and Nancy Crane

The second edition of the best-selling guide to referencing electronic information and citing the complete range of electronic formats includes text-based information, electronic journals and discussion lists, Web sites, CD-ROM and multimedia products, and commercial online documents.

1996/214 pp/softbound • ISBN 1-57387-027-7 • $19.99

For a complete catalog, contact:

Information Today, Inc.

143 Old Marlton Pike, Medford, NJ 08055 • 609/654-6266
email: custserv@infotoday.com • Web site: www.infotoday.com